INTERPET
HANDBOOKS

POPULAR
POND
PLANTS

POPULAR
POND
PLANTS

PHILIP SWINDELLS

Howell Book House

591.7

For general information on IDG Books
Worldwide's books in the U.S., please call our
Consumer Customer Service department at
800-762-2974. For reseller information,
including discounts and premium sales, please
call our Reseller Customer Service department
at 800-434-3422.

Credits
Created and designed: Ideas into Print.
Artwork: Guy Smith, Mainline Design.
Production management: Consortium.
Print production: Sino Publishing House Ltd.
Printed and bound in China.

The author
Philip Swindells has more than 30 years of
practical professional horticultural experience
and now acts as a consultant specializing in
the conservation, restoration and management
of historic gardens, particularly water gardens.

Below: Nymphaea 'A.O. Siebert'.

Contents

PART ONE

The role of pond plants

It is possible to have a water garden without pond plants, providing it is filtered and artificially treated to control algae. There are some very fine water features throughout the world, with spectacular fountains and cascades that display the skills of engineers, but have little to do with water gardening. Water gardening is the art and science of the cultivation of pond plants, together with the care and management of fish and other creatures in an attractive and balanced aquatic environment.

Plants are the most important component in any water gardening enterprise, since it is possible to create a balanced aquatic environment with them alone, but without them a pond is a disaster, unless you set up artificial assistance in the form of a filtration system. When introduced in the right proportions, plants enable a sustainable, harmonious environment to be established in all but the smallest water bodies. Even where a natural ecological balance cannot be achieved because the volume of water is too tiny and temperature rises and falls are dramatic, they still confer benefits.

In purely practical terms, plants (particularly submerged ones) are essential in producing clear healthy water; they mop up the excess nutrients, thereby starving out green, water-discolouring algae. When submerged plants are insufficient, you can allow the spread of surface foliage to extend so that the water is shaded beneath. This prevents the algae from surviving and, as long as there is sufficient light penetration to enable the submerged aquatics to function properly, makes a major contribution to water clarity and purity.

This part of the book explores the practical aspects of using pond plants, from choosing and planting to propagation, pests and diseases.

CREATING A WATER GARDEN

There are many things to consider when introducing a water feature to a garden, not only design elements but also practical aspects to ensure its continued success. Take all of these into account before construction begins.

The pond environment

Even a small pond, such as this rectangular water feature in a town garden, can support fish and a range of attractive pond plants.

The position of a pool within the garden has a vital bearing on its ultimate well-being. The design, arrangement and how it will fit into the garden landscape is of course important, but before considering those factors you must take into account the welfare of the plants and other aquatic life. If you do not pay due attention to the siting, it may be difficult to create a balanced ecology within the pool. For a water garden to be successful, the plants must flourish and the fish and other livestock must be content.

The vital role of sunlight

For best results, pond plants require a position in full, uninterrupted sunlight, even though this is conducive to a proliferation of green, water-discolouring algae. In such a situation the plants will flourish and compete with the algae, the submerged oxygenating plants using the dissolved nutrients in the water and the floating aquatics reducing the light falling directly beneath the water surface. Together, they make it difficult for primitive plant life, such as algae, to thrive. Prolific plant growth on the surface of the water also provides a refuge for goldfish and other ornamental pond fish, while an abundance of submerged growth ensures that there are favourable spawning conditions.

Overhanging trees
Sunlight is vital if fish and plants are to prosper, and while it might not be possible to provide a site without any shade at all, minimal shade should be a prime consideration. Of course, shade can be created in a number of ways, and while buildings and fences are a nuisance when they cast shadows, they are not as troublesome as overhanging trees. It is trees that pose potentially the greatest hazard, for all have leaves that are to some extent toxic if they fall into the water and start to decompose. This is not only the case in autumn; they often cause problems during the summer, too, especially where the weeping willow is concerned. Although visually appealing – especially beside water – avoid the weeping willow, because its foliage contains an aspirin-like chemical that can be harmful to fish when the leaves are decomposing in the water. Pendulous cherries are sometimes used as a replacement because they have the same desirable habit and are a more appropriate size. However, they and all their decorative and culinary

cousins should also be avoided for waterside planting as they are the overwintering host of the waterlily aphid. The only way to control this difficult pest is to spray host trees with a winter wash to break the life cycle. This is not possible when the tree is in close proximity to a pool.

Soil conditions
Soil conditions can also have a major bearing on the siting of a pool, especially the material from which it is constructed. It is difficult to lay a pond liner on loose sandy soils, but preformed shapes are easier to install. However, the opposite is generally true on heavier soil. The presence of a high water table and the absence of drainage are likely to be the greatest constraining factors. It is often thought that a low, wet place in the garden is ideal for a pool. The reality is very different, as it is often not consistently wet and therefore unsuitable for a natural earth-bottom construction. Similarly, a liner or preformed plastic or glass-reinforced plastic shape will be disrupted by the rising winter water table unless you fundamentally improve the drainage and relieve ground water pressure.

Aesthetic considerations
Apart from practical considerations concerning the cultivation of plants, there are aesthetic aspects to take into account when deciding precisely where to locate a pool. In nature, water is usually found at the lowest point in the landscape, which is where it looks most natural, even when the garden around it is more

formal and manicured. It is unclear why this should be, but it is doubtless related to light and the reflective qualities of the water. A pool positioned higher than the surrounding area always looks ill-at-ease, except in the case of a formal construction where a deliberately raised pool is part of the hard landscape of a garden.

Although it may seem obvious to place a pool at the lowest point in the garden, this may not be practical, perhaps because of seasonal flooding, as we have seen, or the presence of a mature overhanging tree. And it may be far removed from the direct line of sight from the house. So in many cases a compromise will prove necessary. This can best be achieved by the careful redistribution of excavated soil and thereafter the skilful positioning of plants, other than those that are going to be growing in the water. Shrubs, bamboos and other structural plants can make an enormous difference to the overall appearance and setting of the finished pool.

A view of the pond

Whatever the position of the pool in the garden, you should always be able to see its best aspect from what you consider to be the most important viewpoint, whether that be the house, patio or a garden seat. However, bear in mind that whatever you do to accommodate the requirements of the primary viewpoint, this will have an effect on other aspects. You are creating a three-dimensional work of art that

will be observed with varying degrees of frequency from different angles, so the aim is to put the best face on each one. While the structure of the pool can have a considerable influence on this, it is the arrangement of the plants that plays the greatest part. To some extent, a garden pond is a stage and the plants are the actors upon it.

The bog garden

Apart from the main body of the pool itself, in informal situations an extended boggy area can be a natural floral bonus. Many pond owners treat a bog garden as an addition, whereas its overall design and

arrangement should be considered from the outset. The same applies to streams and rills, as these can have a considerable visual impact, as well as provide conditions to extend the range of plants being grown. Another advantage is that the season of interest can be extended by including one or two swamp-dwelling shrubs, such as the coloured-stemmed *Cornus alba* 'Sibirica' and its cousin

Below: A reflective pool provides a lovely setting for groups of waterlilies, but it is the submerged plants working beneath the surface that ensure an ecological balance and water clarity. The pond looks good from all angles, especially the seat.

Cornus stolonifera 'Flaviramea', together with the swamp blueberry, *Vaccinium corymbosum*. Bog garden plants can add interest to the pond area from spring until late summer, but these shrubby plants – especially the cornus with their brightly coloured stems – can extend the season of interest through the winter.

All bog garden plants, with the exception of one or two ferns, require similar conditions to pond plants. Provide an open, sunny position with consistent moisture but no waterlogging. Ferns, such as the osmunda, or royal fern, will tolerate shade, as will the sensitive and ostrich-feather ferns.

Plant requirements under water

The aesthetics of a water garden largely result from the juxtaposition of the plants with the open area of water. Whether this is successfully achieved depends very much on the facilities for plant growth and development determined by the unseen pond profile. The provision of suitable growing areas beneath the water have a considerable influence on how the pool appears at the surface. With regard to this, there are four groups of plants to consider, each with its own requirements for successful cultivation.

Waterlilies and deep water aquatics

The waterlilies and other deep water aquatics, such as water hawthorn *(Aponogeton distachyos)* and water fringe *(Nymphoides peltata)*, require deeper water than marginal plants. Rarely does this need to be more than 90cm (36in), as all the most popular varieties of waterlily will

Above: The deep water aquatics, such as this water hawthorn (Aponogeton distachyos), *provide an attractive and often fragrant display, but also contribute to the balance of the pool by providing essential surface shade.*

grow satisfactorily in that depth of water. This is also the maximum depth at which other deep water aquatics will grow happily. A successful ecological balance within a garden pond does not depend on an excessive depth of water, but on a sensible balance for aquatic life between depth and surface area.

Where a shallower pool is unavoidable, it is possible to select waterlily varieties that are happier in shallower water. Some of the pygmy varieties will flourish in as little as 15cm (6in) of water, while most deep water aquatics are tolerant of as little as 30cm (12in), although they do not develop as freely and attractively when constrained in this way.

Submerged aquatics

Submerged aquatics must have a sufficient depth of water in which to remain submerged in a water temperature that does not become too high during summer. Hot, shallow water leads to their discolouring and disintegration. The majority of popular submerged aquatics grow best in water 45-90cm (18-36in) deep. In deeper water they start to struggle, as conditions are dark and gloomy and not conducive to healthy growth. Although few are of any significance when in flower, the majority of submerged plants do break the water surface at flowering time. The length of their stems is dictated by the depth of the water in the pond. Providing that this is no greater than 90cm (36in), there is unlikely to be any impediment to natural plant development.

Floating plants

Floating plants are not concerned about the depth of water, providing that they can float about freely. However, bear in mind that the winter buds, or turions, of a plant such as the frogbit *(Hydrocharis morsus-ranae)* overwinter on the floor of the pond. In deep water, it is going to take longer for the water to warm and stir them into growth than would be the case in a shallower body of water. To counter this, gather a few buds during the autumn and overwinter them in a washing-up bowl with a layer of soil on the bottom and filled with water. Place the bowl in a cool, frost-free but light position until early spring.

Marginal plants

Marginal shelves and areas allow you to grow plants with a water depth requirement ranging from moist soil to 20cm (8in) of water. While growing plants in containers is widely advocated, there are occasions where direct planting into soil scattered along marginal areas or indeed in natural earth-bottomed ponds is preferable. In such cases the profiling of the areas to be planted can have a great influence on the ultimate shape and configuration of the planting, the spread of the plants being controlled by the underwater profile of the pond.

Above: Flexible containers – here planted with cyperus and lobelia – can be gently wedged onto marginal shelves. Place a layer of fine gravel on top of the basket.

Formal planting

The principles behind formal water gardens are rigid and mathematical and also depend a great deal on visual balance. Open water plays an important part, often more significant than that of the plants, as formality is very much about the art of gardening and the placement of plants and objects. In order to achieve the desired effect, it is essential to have a good knowledge of the plants being used, particularly their habit and behaviour.

Cultivated forms and varieties are the most predictable, because if they have been vegetatively propagated

they are genetically identical and therefore their height, spread and colour should be predictable. (This is assuming that they were grown in a uniform growing medium under identical conditions.) Species are notoriously variable, especially when seed-raised, and they are rarely suitable where well-restrained planting is desired.

Architectural plants

Plants with architectural shapes are generally preferred for formal water features. The distinctively marked zebra rush, *Schoenoplectus lacustris tabernaemontani* 'Zebrinus', and its cousin, the creamy white-stemmed 'Albescens', are outstanding examples. True aquatic irises derived from *Iris laevigata* and *I. versicolor* are also extremely effective, with their well-ordered fans of leaves,

Above: Nymphaea *'Gonnère' is a very fine large, white, double waterlily that will flourish in a medium-sized pond and is well suited to a formal water feature.*

Right: In a formal water garden, architectural marginal aquatic plants, such as the zebra rush (Schoenoplectus lacustris tabernaemontani 'Zebrinus'), provide invaluable height and structure for the mirrorlike surface of the water.

especially the cream-and-green
variegated varieties. The variegated
sweet flag, *Acorus calamus*
'Variegatus', fulfils a similar function.
Its foliage is significantly taller, glossy
and smells of tangerines.

Waterlilies
Waterlilies can be grown formally in
the open water. Choose plants of the
same size and variety where more
than one spread of foliage is
required. Select only named kinds,
avoiding species such as the
European *Nymphaea alba* and North
American *N. tuberosa*. In order to
obtain an even foliage coverage, take
great care to select a variety that will
cope with the depth of water in your
pond. If the water is too shallow, the

*Above: Irises are wonderful plants in all
settings, their bold architectural fans of
leaves creating valuable contrasts to the
less formal hummocks of other plants,
such as marsh marigolds and bog bean.*

waterlily leaves will often pile up out
of the water, whereas if it is too deep,
the plants will struggle and uneven
groups of yellowing or sickly looking
leaves will populate the surface.

Scented plants
Formal pools are often a feature of
an enclosed area, such as a
courtyard, and here there is an
opportunity to take advantage of
fragrance, as well as colour and
habit. Scents tend to linger in the
warm, still atmosphere of an

enclosed space and make a significant additional contribution to poolside enjoyment. Select a fragrant waterlily, such as the aniseed-scented 'Rose Arey', or plant water hawthorn *(Aponogeton distachyos)*, with its cloying vanilla fragrance. And do not neglect those aquatics with scented leaves, especially where the pool is raised and the foliage is more readily available to the touch.

Oriental ponds

Of course, formality can take on many different guises and while most formal ponds follow traditional Western ideas, the Orient has a lot to offer. With the burgeoning interest in keeping koi (coloured varieties of the common carp), oriental themes have become very popular and fashionable. These depend heavily upon the combination of landscape materials, such as cobbles, paving, rocks and gravel, and very specific planting, which in its original concept has a very precise meaning. For most pond owners it is the visual effect that is a priority, underlying meanings being interesting but not essential. Ponds such as these usually feature truly oriental plants, such as the dwarf Japanese reedmace *(Typha minima)*, but providing a plant has a hint of the Orient about it there is no reason not to use it.

Left: This formal pool
with a flagstone path
surround gains much
from the reflective
mirrorlike quality of
open water. The
statuesque irises frame
the water spout.

Right: The dwarf Japanese reedmace
(Typha minima) *is one of the finest
marginal aquatic plants for the
oriental-style water garden, making
a significant contribution to pools
both large and small.*

*Dwarf Japanese
reedmace has
attractive dark
brown seedheads.*

Left: Bamboo artifacts,
such as this deer scarer,
or shishi-odoshi, even
if they are not always
fully functional, add a
touch of realism to
modern western
oriental gardens.

Informal planting

While the arrangement of plants in a pond is a very personal matter, the visual aspect of the water is crucial. With an informally planted pool you might think that because the plants do not appear to conform to a predetermined pattern, it is simple to create a pleasing display. Nothing could be further from the truth; producing a planting arrangement that is successful, well balanced and simple to manage demands considerable skill, because the plants have to look cared for, but without any evidence of manicuring.

Above: Although an informal planting looks easy to create and maintain, it requires great care and thought to make it appear natural and at the same time produce an ecological balance.

Using planting baskets

Planting baskets help to resolve the situation, because plants that are pleasing to the eye when grown next to each other can happily coexist in separate baskets without the fear that one will invade the other's territory. The disadvantage is that the configuration of the container is formal and the arrangement of plants has to take this into account. Some ingenuity is required to ensure that everything comes together harmoniously, perhaps occasional dual plantings in a basket to soften the edges.

When using stiff, upright plants, such as zebra rush *(Schoenoplectus lacustris tabernaemontani* 'Zebrinus'), there is no difficulty in

Below: Yellow marsh marigolds contrast with vivid candelabra primulas to create a striking streamside planting. This mix of marginal and bog plants exploits their simultaneous flowering period.

adding a sprawling plant, such as the water forget-me-not *(Myosotis scorpioides).* Neither plant has an invasive root system and with compatible growth rates they can live together harmoniously. Such combinations can be very valuable, especially in a small pool, but take care not to overdo them in a larger water feature, otherwise the effect will be one of developing formality.

Plant associations
When arranging plants in an informal water feature, especially marginal and bog garden subjects,

apply the same considerations as you would to a mixed flower border. Take account of flowering periods and any opportunities for creating pleasing contrasts and combinations of character and colour. Cotton grass *(Eriophorum angustifolium)* and the water forget-me-not *(Myostis scorpioides)* always combine happily, as do the North American pickerel *(Pontederia cordata)* and the European flowering rush *(Butomus umbellatus)*. Bog bean *(Menyanthes trifoliata)* makes a pretty picture while scrambling amongst the common marsh marigold *(Caltha palustris)*, and the architectural quality of the golden-variegated, swordlike foliage of *Iris pseudacorus* 'Variegatus' contrasts starkly with

the scrambling, glossy, evergreen leaves of the bog arum *(Calla palustris)*, with its elegant, sail-like white blossoms.

Choosing waterlilies

Within the water, combinations and associated plantings are not so desirable, as waterlilies and other deep water aquatics are best seen alone, surrounded by crystal clear water. Thus the careful choice of variety, especially with waterlilies, is crucial for the best results. Select a well-tried and reliable commercial variety as the centrepiece. Be wary of some of the modern untried varieties, because although they may have performed well in trials in the pools of their originators, the majority of

modern hardy waterlilies have been developed in warm climates. Although they should theoretically prosper in cooler temperate conditions, they often do not flower as freely. Always consider a new variety as an adjunct to the main display until it has proved itself beyond doubt in its new home.

Growing plants in containers

Although it is desirable to have a pond in which to grow aquatic plants, it is by no means essential, as the majority of popular plants will grow successfully in a container or tub. Indeed, for the aquatic plant collector there is probably some merit in this method of cultivation, as in most cases it is better to grow a single plant in a container, especially where waterlilies are concerned. This enables you to study the beauty, habit and behaviour of the plant without impediment.

For most gardeners, the container water garden offers an opportunity to grow aquatic plants in places where it is impossible to construct a pond. It provides a chance to grow pygmy plants in a more appropriate setting, especially tiny waterlilies and the dwarf Japanese reedmace (*Typha minima*). Indeed, the conditions offered by tub culture are even better for pygmy waterlilies than the conventional pool margin where they are normally accommodated.

Pygmy waterlilies in containers

Pygmy waterlilies are derived from species that in their natural habitat often dwell in small shallow bodies of water that dry up for part of the year. They are, therefore, very resilient and quite adaptable to a period of dormancy, when they will survive just-damp conditions. Thus, when grown in a tub or half-barrel they can be dried off for the winter without coming to any harm, providing that the planting mixture does not dry out completely. This is extremely useful, because instead of a gloomy tub full of water on the patio for the winter months, the water can be drained off and the tub stored away in a shed or garage, complete with mud and waterlily.

Of course, you can add other plants to a tub containing a pygmy waterlily, but choose them carefully to avoid an overplanted appearance. You must accept that it is impossible to create a natural balance within such a confined water body, so avoid submerged aquatics. Their well-meaning introduction into containers usually results in tangled congestion. Simplicity is what is required to achieve the best visual effect.

Sinks as containers

Apart from tubs and containers, sinks are very popular for small-growing aquatic plants. From the point of view of cultivation, you can regard them rather like tubs, although they do lend themselves to the creation of miniature waterscapes. Once again, simplicity is the key to creating a satisfactory effect. One or two pieces of rock positioned so that they break the surface of the water form a pleasing infrastructure. Fill the gaps between the rocks and the edge of the sink with aquatic soil for planting. When selecting rocks for a miniature waterscape, avoid sandstone and limestone as they often crumble when subjected to prolonged immersion in water.

Choose plants carefully, selecting varieties that will not swamp the sink completely, but acknowledge that because of the restricted conditions replanting will be necessary every spring. Only refurbish the sink during spring, allowing the plants to overwinter undisturbed, even if they look a little untidy. Trying to smarten up the planting before the winter will result in heavy plant losses.

Below: Pygmy waterlilies, such as these Nymphaea *'Pygmaea Helvola' and* N. *'Pygmaea Rubra', and the dwarf Japanese reedmace* (Typha minima) *are excellent companions for a tub garden.*

Planting for wildlife

Although a wildlife pool looks informal and easy to manage, of all the water features it is the one that has to be most carefully planned. This may seem surprising, since the most successful wildlife water features look as if they have occurred naturally, growing in an unruly, yet controlled manner. However, to achieve this result, you have to understand how the plants behave. While attracting wildlife is the main objective, it should not be the overriding factor when it comes to selecting plants. The majority of native species normally recommended for the garden pond will attract wildlife, so there is quite a wide range of plants to choose from in terms of growth habit and behaviour. If you hope to attract a

Below: Once pool planting becomes established, a wide range of wildlife will arrive quite naturally. Frogs are amongst the most regular and useful inhabitants, feeding on slugs and insects.

particular insect or butterfly, you can strategically incorporate the host plant without affecting the overall planting scheme.

Arranging plants

Visually, it seldom matters which plants are arranged adjacent to one another, providing that their growth rates are similar. Most native wildlife plants are much less striking in appearance than their garden relatives, so the prospect of stark colour contrasts is remote. The arrangement of plants also has little bearing upon how wildlife will populate them, as specific creatures will target host plants wherever they are growing in the pool.

Planting in baskets

The planting method you choose will have a major influence on the type of planting arrangements possible. From the plant management point of view, planting baskets are the simplest option. Most native aquatic plants are vigorous and will quickly invade one another's territory. Container cultivation reduces the risk of such a nuisance. However, using baskets is not the easiest way to achieve visual success in a planted pool.

Plants with vigorous root systems, such as the reedmaces and bur reeds (*Sparganium erectum* and *S. minimum*), must be contained as far as possible. Planting baskets are less than ideal for tall-growing plants, such as *Typha latifolia*, as fully grown plants topple into the water at the slightest breeze unless safely secured below. When there is room, wire two or three baskets together and plant the typhas so that their roots can pass through the latticework sides and invade one another. This creates greater stability.

Planting submerged aquatics
If you intend carpeting the floor of an artificial pool, plant submerged aquatic plants in plastic seed trays, rather than covering the bottom of the pool with soil or gravel and planting into that. Fill the trays with aquatic planting mixture or gravel and introduce several bunches of submerged aquatics to each tray. Place all the trays abutting each other on the pool floor and the plants will eventually provide an underwater carpet of foliage that is easy to retrieve when you carry out regular pond maintenance.

Planting directly into the pool
Planting directly into the pool creates all manner of management problems, especially amongst vigorous reeds and rushes. No matter what you start with in spring, by midsummer everything will be in a tangle. With large water features this may be acceptable, but it is difficult to cope with in the domestic wildlife pool.

Below: Carefully planned planting is necessary in order to create a balanced wildlife pool. An area of open water is essential for many aquatic creatures.

Right: Although not important in creating a display, submerged aquatic plants are vital in establishing a natural ecological balance. They utilise the nutrients on which water-discolouring algae depend.

Left: Shading the water surface with floating foliage helps to create a balance environment, but permanent shade from trees is detrimental to pond life and the successful cultivation of aquatic plants.

Creating a natural balance

To ensure a trouble-free pond, it is necessary to create a natural ecological balance. This provides a happy home for all the aquatic inhabitants and guarantees water clarity. Once all the necessary components have been introduced, a balance will usually be maintained. It is only when one element fails that problems start to occur.

It is easier to create a natural balance from the planting of a pool, than to try to correct it later. There are no hard-and-fast rules to follow when stocking the pool initially, but it is worth adhering to some basic principles that will help you to achieve a satisfactory balance. These have been interpreted into rough-and-ready guidelines by pondkeepers and seem to work well in all but the tiniest of ponds.

The role of submerged plants

There are several important aspects to consider when creating a natural balance. The most crucial one is the role of the submerged aquatic plants. Their main function is to use up the nutrients in the water, and during the daytime to provide oxygen for fish and other pond life. They are also a food source for fish and provide a home for aquatic insect life, which in turn is part of the pond's larder for the fish. Fine-leaved kinds also provide a suitable place for the deposition of fish spawn and a relatively safe home for the young fry during their early life.

From the outset, their main role is to mop up excessive nutrients in the water, thereby reducing the occurrence of water-discolouring algae. It is suspended single-celled algae that can turn the pond water into the consistency of pea soup, obscuring the fish and in due course leaving an unsightly deposit on the foliage of submerged plants. In the plant kingdom, submerged aquatic plants are higher forms of life than algae, and if they are established in sufficient numbers, they will dominate and starve out the algae by using all the nutrients upon which the algae would normally feed.

Shading the pond

Sunlight also encourages green water. Nutrient-rich water in full sun will soon display a strong algal bloom. Algae, like most other aquatic plant life, enjoys full sun, so its incidence can be reduced by shading the water. First thoughts may be to shade the pool by planting trees and shrubs in close proximity, but this is not a good idea, as it will restrict the proper growth of waterlilies and decorative marginal aquatics. The answer is to provide shade on the surface of the water itself, using a combination of floating aquatic plants and waterlily foliage. This only affects plants – including the algae within the pool – and has no bearing on the performance of the emergent aquatics.

Other plants, fish and snails

Marginal aquatics have little effect on the balance within the pool, providing they are grown in proper aquatic planting mixture and in reasonably sized containers. They then take full advantage of the nutrients present and do not add to the burden of the submerged aquatics in deeper water. Fish also assist in maintaining a balance, particularly by controlling aquatic insect pests, although they make a contribution with their waste to the nutrition of the plants. Ramshorn snails can also be added, as they assist in the control of filamentous algae, or blanketweed.

Balanced planting

Having grasped the principles of creating a natural balance, it becomes evident that the pondkeeper must consider the planting implications for the well-being of the pool in advance of making specific plant selections. It is worth categorising the plant types required and then matching your selections to the roles that they are going to perform in the completed pond.

How many plants will I need?

To put together a planting plan, calculate the surface area of the pond (multiply the length by the width excluding the marginal shelves) and plant nine bunches of submerged aquatics per square metre (about a square yard), irrespective of the depth of the water. Put each group of nine plants of one species in a single aquatic basket. They do not have to

be distributed evenly over the floor of the pool. It is the relationship of plant quantity to total surface area that is important.

Using the same calculation for the surface area, allow for the waterlilies and other deep water aquatics to cover about one-third of the surface area. This is quite difficult to assess in advance, as there are considerable variations within varieties, especially amongst the waterlilies. The quality of the water and aquatic soil can also affect their performance. But there is some leeway in the calculation and providing the ultimate water surface cover does not exceed half, the submerged plants will still perform satisfactorily, while suspended algae will find life intolerable.

The role of fish

Fish play an essential role in the pool, even if you are preoccupied with the plants. Apart from keeping many aquatic insect pests under control, they also eliminate troublesome mosquito larvae. It is important that there are sufficient fish present, but not an over-population; too many fish may start to damage the plants or add excessive nutrients to the water with their natural waste. Using the same surface area calculation, permit no more than 45cm (18in) length of fish for each square metre (or square

Right: Moving water is a most attractive feature, but it does preclude the successful cultivation of many of the best aquatic plants, which are naturally inhabitants of quiet backwaters.

yard) of surface area. When calculating the length of fish, include the tail and use whatever combination of numbers and lengths suits best, but do not exceed the total length of fish stated. This will allow the fish to grow and develop, but at the same time ensures a gradual and naturally evolving balance.

Snails in the pond

Snails of the ramshorn variety can be added at will, for if there ever appears to be an over-population, the fish usually take them in hand, regarding the succulent flat pads of jelly containing the eggs as a delicacy.

Choosing submerged aquatics

When choosing plants in order to create a balance, always select a few very reliable kinds to mix with those that are perhaps more fickle and often more attractive. This is especially important with submerged aquatics. Many, such as milfoils and water crowfoot, disappear almost completely for the winter, reappearing in the spring when the water starts to warm up. Often by this time, the fast-growing, single-celled algae have started to invade, clouding the water and cutting out light to the awakening submerged aquatics. To counter this, include at least one evergreen species, such the curled pondweed *(Potamogeton crispus)* or Canadian pondweed *(Elodea canadensis)*. They look a little scruffy during the winter, but will be as quick off the mark in the spring as the single-celled algae and will usually keep them under control.

Tropical pond plants

In regions with a consistently warm summer climate, you can grow a variety of exotic tropical pond plants. However, bear in mind that these are not frost tolerant and must also have high summer temperatures if they are to prosper. Where winters are warm, the plants can be allowed to remain in the pool, otherwise they must be over-wintered indoors. Alternatively, try growing them in a greenhouse or conservatory all year round.

Below: Tropical waterlilies are available in a much wider range of colours than the hardy varieties. They can be either day-blooming or nocturnal flowering.

Above: *The sacred lotus* (Nelumbo nucifera) *is amongst the finest tropical aquatic plants. There are many different varieties available, from the dwarf tea cup lotus to the giant seat of Buddha.*

Right: *Thalia dealbata, an exotic-looking tropical marginal plant that flourishes in hot climates, also puts on a creditable summer display in cool, temperate areas. It is not frost hardy.*

35

USING POND PLANTS

A water garden is only as successful as its plants. Unlike other garden features, a pond is a completely self-contained environment in which the plants play a crucial role. Look after them and the reward is clear water and a fine display.

Choosing and buying plants

Nowadays, most pond plants are bought in containers from nurseries or garden centres rather than by mail order. In recent years, nurserymen have developed much better techniques of producing attractive saleable plants in planters, and the water garden section of retail nursery outlets is generally as well organised as the trees, shrubs and border plants. However, for the slightly more unusual varieties, or if you are seeking plants in quantity, mail order is still the most favoured option.

Giving plants a good start

Cut back deep water aquatic plants, such as the water fringe (*Nymphoides peltata*), before planting them. They soon produce fresh, vigorous growth.

Instant impact

Mail-order plants are available from spring until late summer, but if you want to create something of a display in the first year, buy freshly sprouting plants early in the season. Pond plants grow very quickly and by early summer most of them require cutting back when they are being planted if die-back is not to occur. Not that this die-back is damaging to such plants, it is just very untidy.

Bare-rooted plants
Fresh, nursery-lifted plants that are sold bare-rooted almost always require cutting back, even very early in the year. When you buy by mail order, there is not really much opportunity to choose plants other than by variety, so you are dependent on your supplier to provide plants of good quality and size. However, early in the season this is not always easy for the customer to judge, as certain plants, such as frogbit *(Hydrocharis morsus-ranae)* and arrowhead *(Sagittaria sagittifolia)*, are naturally very tiny at first. Nevertheless, they will produce quality plants during the summer. If you are unsure about what you are going to get, it is probably better to wait until later in the season when the plants are actively growing. Providing that plants are clean, fresh, well-washed and devoid of the sticky cylinders of jelly containing the eggs of the greater pond snail (see pages 40 and 71), then they should establish well. None of them need be potgrown to avoid root disturbance, as is the case with many garden plants.

Plants from the garden centre
Selecting potgrown plants from a garden centre display is much easier. It is quite clear what you are buying, and providing that plants are fresh, established in pots or planters and true to name, they can be transferred to the home pool without any fuss.

Avoid buying pond plants early in the season, when the garden centre is anxious to promote sales of good leafy plants. Wholesale growers often force plants into premature growth with the protection of a tunnel. This certainly brings the plants on quickly, but does not fit them for early establishment outdoors in the pond. It may be clearer to see what the plants are going to look like, but such plants may not be the best investments in the long run.

What to look for
Container-grown pond plants should look fresh and not forced into growth. They should not have been

Above: The taller plant is a fine specimen with vigorous healthy foliage. The smaller, poor specimen is potbound and starved, and probably considerably older than its companion. With care, it should recover.

To be certain that the soil structure is suitable, take a trowelful and dry it out thoroughly. Break it down into a powder and then mix it with water in a clean, empty, glass jar. Allow the soil to settle out over a period of two or three days. The sand will sink quickly to the bottom, while the clay particles will form a layer on top. Providing that this comprises 75% of the sample, then the soil is acceptable for the cultivation of pond plants.

established in their pots so long that they have become stunted and jaded. It is true that they will usually grow if their roots are teased out and trimmed and they are relieved of their constraint, but this recovery can often take the whole season.

Submerged aquatics are less likely to be grown in pots. The majority are sold in bunches fastened together with a strip of lead. The foliage of underwater plants should always be fresh and show no signs of browning or other discoloration.

Soils and planting mixtures

Although you can buy specially prepared aquatic planting mixtures, good, clean garden soil can be satisfactorily used for growing pond plants. The main requirement for success is to understand the ecology of the pond and the nutritional needs of the plants. The constituents of a growing medium can have a marked effect on the clarity and chemistry of the pool, so it is essential to look at this aspect before considering the plants' requirements.

A balanced growing medium should be of a heavy structure, ideally a clay or heavy clay loam. This consists of minute, evenly sized particles that cling together and do not readily disperse into the water.

Preparing garden soil for planting

When gardening on a light or medium-light loam soil, you must use specially manufactured aquatic planting mixture. On heavier land there is a choice, as it is not difficult to create a perfectly acceptable aquatic plant growing medium from garden soil if it has not recently been dressed with an artificial fertilizer.

When digging the soil, remove obvious weeds and any other coarse organic matter that will decompose and pollute the water. Discard large stones and pass the soil through a garden sieve placed over a wheelbarrow. This will retain any undesirable debris, such as sticks and pieces of glass or china, leaving a heap of finely graded soil. Use the soil just as it is, without adding any fertilizer. Feed pond plants using specially manufactured slow-release fertilizer tablets or perforated sachets of granular feed (see page 53).

Organic matter

Organic matter is appreciated by the plants but is not an essential requirement. This is fortunate, given that it has the potential to cause pollution problems as it decomposes in the water. Sufficient organic matter accumulates naturally in a pond from fallen leaves and in the decomposing aquatic vegetation, without adding to the problem in the planting mixture.

Organic matter decomposes and produces noxious gases, which under normal circumstances escape freely into the atmosphere without upsetting the balance of the pond.

However, during winter when the water is iced over, it becomes trapped and can asphyxiate the fish, so during a prolonged period of cold the ice should be vented. Under spring and summer conditions, an excess of organic matter in the pool will also release an excess of nutrients, which may lead to an abundant growth of algae.

When preparing a suitable growing medium for aquatic plants, make sure that it contains sufficient nutrients for the plants that are going to grow in it, but there is not the potential for leaching into the water and the development of algal bloom.

Planting baskets and mixtures

Aquatic planting baskets with micromesh or lattice-work sides are available in a range of shapes and sizes.

Specially formulated aquatic planting mixture.

A layer of fine pea gravel spread over the planted basket deters fish from digging and prevents soil dispersing into the water.

Preparing plants for planting

Pond plants can be successfully planted from late spring until late summer. For a respectable show in the first season, you must get the plants into the pond before midsummer. Although later plantings establish well, they have to be cut hard back before planting and consequently look ugly for much of the remainder of the season.

The greater pond snail

Freshly bought or divided plants can usually be planted without much preparation in early spring, but inspect all leafy plants carefully for the cylindrical jelly containing the eggs of the greater pond snail. This snail is very common and even deliberately introduced on occasion, as it is believed to graze on algae. The reality is that it will do so, but much prefers the foliage of waterlilies. Gardeners who suddenly find a population of this snail in their ponds when they have not knowingly introduced it, have probably unwittingly brought it in on plants. Sometimes it goes into the pond unnoticed, but often it is mistaken for goldfish spawn. In fact, the two bear little resemblance.

Cutting back plants

Assess all plants for balance, namely the size of the top in relation to the root. When either is in excess, hard cutting back is essential. Do not be nervous about removing the foliage from any well-rooted aquatic plant. Providing that it is in good health, it will grow away again very quickly.

Preparing waterlilies

Waterlilies often arrive with a disproportionate amount of foliage, especially when they are bare-rooted. If this foliage is allowed to remain after planting, it will usually die. In the meantime, it serves as an aid to buoyancy, lifting the plant right out of the container in which it has been freshly planted. Any flower buds

Left: Cut away the bulk of any fibrous roots, as they will die back in any case. It is a good idea to reduce the length of the foliage in order to create a balanced plant for potting up.

present that are larger than a garden pea are unlikely to develop properly and open. In these cases, it is sensible to cut the foliage right back to the crown and just leave the spearlike, submerged foliage intact. Trim the roots as well, and if there are any signs of decay on the rootstock, pare it back to sound material. Roots, like foliage, are likely to die back when transplanted and are best trimmed back to ensure vigorous regeneration.

Of course, some waterlilies are established in containers when you buy them and theoretically you can position them in the pond without them realising that they have been moved. The reality is somewhat different, for even if the plants are propped up on bricks to ensure that they are at exactly the same level in the water as before, the leaves are likely to curl and no longer lie flat on the water. Again, it is best to remove all floating foliage and flowers and to place the plant at the desirable depth. It is amazing how quickly a growing aquatic plant will refurnish itself with foliage and develop normally.

Preparing marginal plants

Tall-growing marginal plants also require cutting back before planting. Often by midseason they are totally out of proportion to their root system. Do not be nervous about cutting them back vigorously, as they will quickly regrow. Even young plants already established in containers can be encouraged to grow stronger and bushier by prudent trimming back before you put them in position.

Preparing submerged plants

With submerged plants, the more vigorous the young shoots the better. Those of the current season's growth are essential, especially early in the season. When preparing new bunches from existing plants, remove a number of sprigs of healthy growth and wrap a thin strip of lead around the base. Make sure that the lead is completely buried when you plant the bunches, otherwise it will rot through the stems and the cuttings will float to the surface.

Baskets and containers

In a small modern pool or under any circumstances where plants need to be separated and easily controlled, you must use aquatic planting baskets. It is true that container cultivation produces some constraints on growth, but when plants are properly fed and maintained any adverse effects are minimized.

For most aquatic plants, open latticework-sided containers are essential, as they permit the healthy exchange of gases that would be restricted by a solid pot. Waterlilies and other deep water aquatics will grow to begin with in a closed pot or container, but after 18 months or so they start to deteriorate and the growing medium may turn a blackish blue and smell unpleasant. Submerged aquatics are really the only rooting plants that can be successfully grown in closed containers, although it is much better to accommodate them in shallow, open latticework baskets, such as those used for marginal plants.

Plastic baskets

Traditionally, aquatic planting baskets were made from timber and constructed like small crates, although wicker baskets have long been used on large pond projects. Most pondkeepers today use the tough plastic containers. These are available in a range of shapes, sizes and configurations, the better ones being manufactured with micromesh sides to prevent soil spillage into the water. Modern baskets are generally tapered in shape, which helps with the balance of the plants; in high winds, tall reeds or rushes growing in baskets can easily topple over into the water. Plants that are constantly retrieved from the water after a breeze never develop satisfactorily.

Planting into the basket

When planting pond plants in purpose-made aquatic planting baskets, it is usual to line them first with a square of hessian to prevent spillage into the water. With micro-mesh containers this is unnecessary. Loosely fill the container to the top with the growing medium and firmly plant the aquatic as if it were being put into a conventional pot. Take a watering can with a fine rose and soak the planted basket thoroughly. This drives out much of the air from the growing mix and prevents mass bubbling and the possible dirtying of the water when you lower the container into the pool.

Thoroughly watering the basket causes the growing medium to sink. Top it up, firm it by hand and water it heavily until most of the air is

Planting myosotis

1 *Establishing aquatic plants such as myosotis successfully depends on using the correct soil and a suitable container. Use a micromesh basket and aquatic mix or heavy garden soil.*

4 *Water thoroughly to drive all the air out of the soil before placing the basket into the pond. This prevents vigorous bubbling and the distribution of soil and debris into the water.*

USING POND PLANTS

2 Remove the plant carefully from its pot and tease out the roots if the rootball is congested. Make a suitably sized hole in the soil and place the plant in the centre of the basket.

3 Use a trowel to place more soil around the plant and firm it in, leaving sufficient room for a topdressing of well-washed pea gravel. The soil level will drop when you water the basket.

5 Distribute pea gravel over the surface of the soil to prevent fish from stirring it up and dirtying the water. The gravel also adds an attractive finishing touch to the planted basket.

6 Once planted, thoroughly soak the container again using a watering can with a fine rose. This helps to prevent disturbance when the planted basket is lowered into the pond.

Planting Caltha palustris

1 This flexible container is easier to wedge into tight corners than rigid baskets. Part-fill it with soil, make a hole, spread the roots and firm in the plant.

2 Water freely to drive all the air out of the soil. This prevents any air bubbling out and possible escape of soil when the container goes into the pool.

3 Place well-washed pea gravel around the plant, covering the entire surface. This helps to prevent fish from stirring up the soil and clouding the water.

4 Soak the planted basket again before placing it in the pool. All the air should have been excluded and any dust on the gravel washed out.

driven out and the soil or aquatic mix is within 1-2cm (0.4-0.8in) of the surface of the basket. Top off with a layer of fine pea gravel and water again. The gravel will prevent fish from stirring up the soil in their quest for tasty aquatic insect life, such as gnat larvae.

Once the baskets have been prepared they can be placed in position in the pond. While there is often discussion about the virtues of gradually lowering leafy waterlilies into the water and raising them on bricks until their leaf stems extend in order to permit them to be placed in their final lower positions, in reality it is simpler to cut off the emergent leaves and to place the plants in their final position. The new leaves will soon find their own level.

Planting on the pool floor

It would seem quite natural to plant aquatics directly onto the floor of the pool or marginal shelves, as this is how they would grow in Nature. However, the reality of the situation is quite different and such a practice would only be viable in certain very carefully thought-out circumstances.

Many pond plants are vigorous growers and quite invasive. If unrestricted, the faster-growing kinds rapidly overtake the more moderate species. A pond can lose up to half the diversity of plants originally introduced within three years, because the stronger kinds smother the weaker-growing varieties. Often, the most vigorous plants, such as typha and sparganium, will creep beneath or over any solid barrier

used to separate the species. In some circumstances, they may even puncture the pool liner with their sharply pointed rhizomes or creeping rootstocks. This is a particular risk where the pond is lined with a polythene (polyethylene) or PVC liner. By restricting these species to proper aquatic planting baskets such problems can be eliminated.

Regular maintenance

The other major problem for pond owners who plant aquatic plants directly into the pond is coping with cleaning out when this is necessary. A well-ordered and balanced pond planted in this way requires draining down every year to thin out the plants. Periodically, say every four to five years, it will need cleaning out completely. In a natural earth-bottomed or concrete pond this is not going to present any serious difficulties, but it is a very different matter for a pond made with a liner, where every move could unwittingly create a leak. Growing aquatic plants in baskets that can be readily lifted and removed for maintenance is absolutely essential.

Large ponds

Although it is not a good idea to plant directly into the pool in a domestic water garden, the same cannot be said for larger areas of water. This is especially true of naturally occurring ponds planted with native species that attract wildlife. However, because the scale is larger, it does not mean that the plants are any less troublesome; it is just that you can take precautions to control their enthusiasm. If instigated from the outset, these precautions need not disrupt the pond's ecology during routine maintenance.

Controlling vigorous marginals

The first step is to designate the areas where plants are to grow and to control the depth of the water in these areas. Vigorous marginal plants, such as many of the reeds and rushes, can be effectively controlled by planting them in designated shallow areas with very abrupt and steep sides towards open water. By creating sweeps and arcs to the edges of the planting areas, you can create some pleasing visual arrangements of marginal plants.

Planting in open water

In larger areas of open water, it is difficult to plant waterlilies, pond lilies and water hawthorn other than by boat or by walking into the water with chest waders. The planting methods used in the garden are impractical, so the usual method is to wrap the crowns of the plants in squares of hessian, together with a generous quantity of good, clean garden soil or aquatic planting mixture, rather like a parcel. Tie each package around the top with string, leaving the young shoots of each plant just emerging. Then gently

Right: The spread of marginals, such as Schoenoplectus lacustris tabernaemontani *'Albescens', in a natural bottom pond can be controlled by the depth of the water. Deep water creates a barrier to invasion.*

lower each package into the water. Once settled on the bottom, they will root through into the mud on the pond floor and become established. The hessian will eventually rot away.

General care and maintenance
If a water garden is to function satisfactorily, it will require a certain amount of maintenance. Plants need manicuring and the water level needs constant monitoring and adjusting to compensate for evaporation. Apart from this, there are various other tasks involved in the well-being of the plants. Managing a water feature is rather like caring for a large mixed border in its variety.

Immediately the winter has passed, remove any lingering plant remains and mulch the bog garden with well-composted bark or peat. Mulching with organic matter every year helps to improve the soil conditions, but it must not be rich in nutrients, otherwise they will leach into the pool and cause the development of an algal bloom.

Topdressing and inspecting plants
While aquatic plants would not benefit from a traditional mulch, it is a good idea to go around all the containers and topdress them with pea gravel. Inspect the plants at the same time to see whether they are ready for division and remove any stray shoots that are emerging erratically from the baskets. While the plants are being prepared for their growing season, clean out the pool if necessary. In a well-ordered pool this is likely to be a very

infrequent occurrence. Most last for seven to ten years before they need to be drained down.

Plant care during pond cleaning
When this proves to be necessary, make arrangements to keep the plant containers wet. Only the submerged aquatics and waterlilies need be completely submerged in water while the cleaning out is taking place. However, before you consider draining the pond, take the precaution of saving and

Above: *When the flowers have faded, it is prudent to remove the flower stem at the base of the plant. This is* Butomus umbellatus. *Unnecessary seed production of any decorative plant uses energy and reduces vigour. Seedheads should only remain when the seed is to be harvested.*

Below: Once winter has come to the water garden, be sure to remove all poolside debris, including fading leaves and flower stalks, to deprive pests such as the waterlily beetle of an overwintering home. Apart from the fading foliage of waterlilies, do not allow any other vegetation to decompose in the water. In winter, an accumulation of noxious gases resulting from the decomposition of vegetation on the pool floor can become trapped beneath a layer of ice and may asphyxiate the fish.

overwintering the turions, or winter buds, of floating plants, such as frogbit. Rescue these in the autumn, just before their leaves fade and they fall to the pool floor. Place them in a glass jar or bowl of water with a layer of soil in the bottom. In a light, frost-free place, such as the garden shed or garage, they will keep well until the spring.

Summer care

Apart from fertilizing the plants in summer, it is usually necessary to thin out weakly shoots, remove fading foliage and deadhead blossoms before they have an opportunity to set seed. This is very important with some plants, such as water plantain (*Alisma plantago-aquatica*), for not only is seed production a drain on the plant's resources, but if viable seed is produced and scattered by the plant, the emerging seedlings can create a troublesome weed problem. This can be very much the case with some of the reeds and rushes, too.

Submerged aquatics

Observe submerged aquatic plants carefully. Providing a balance has been struck and the water within the pool is clear, regularly remove unsightly surplus growth, together with any elderly, woody material. Avoid carrying out any wholesale clearing of submerged aquatic plants during the summer period, but a little manicuring can make all the difference to the appearance of the pool.

Floating plants

The same principles apply to floating plants, especially the potentially invasive azolla, or fairy moss. This is a great plant if it can be controlled, contributing considerably to ensuring clear water. However, if it is netted off the pool to excess, then the clarity of the water may be affected. It often sticks to the surface of marginal containers and can be a nuisance, so float it off by temporarily raising the water level of the pool.

Left: Filamentous algae can be a nuisance, even in a well-balanced pool where the water is clear. Removing algae by twisting it around a stick is the best method of control, although chemical algicides are also available.

Above: *Azolla, a rapidly growing floating plant, does require regularly thinning out with a net. An excess of shade beneath the water will not only control algae, but will also reduce the growth and efficiency of submerged aquatics.*

Lifting, dividing, replanting and fertilising

All aquatic plants need to be replaced on a regular basis, usually by division or cuttings. Not all grow at the same rate, even amongst related plant groups, so it is difficult to provide general instructions. The more vigorous waterlilies need dividing every three years or so, while some of the smaller-growing and pygmy kinds will last for five or six years if regularly fed and topdressed.

Dividing waterlilies

A waterlily or other deep water aquatic requires lifting and dividing when there is a preponderance of smaller than typical leaves, together with sparse or a total absence of flowering. In the case of waterlilies, particularly the stronger-growing kinds, this is often accompanied by central clusters of leaves that climb out of the water. When such indicators are present, divide the plants quickly. However, if they occur later on in the season, it is often prudent to leave it until the spring of the following year.

Marginal plant care

Marginal plants can be regarded rather like herbaceous perennial border subjects and lifted as necessary. There is a wide discrepancy between the growth rates of, say, a vigorous typha or reedmace and the more pedestrian development of lysichiton, or skunk cabbage. Once you have identified an overcrowded plant, remove it from the pond and divide it, ideally during the spring.

Above: Most marginal aquatic plants make a better display if several of the same variety are planted together in a single large basket.

This gives the plant an opportunity to develop into a reasonably attractive proposition during the current season. Splitting it up once growth is underway not only results in a less pleasing plant visually, but often impairs flowering as well.

Dividing irises

The only plants that require dividing during the summer are the irises. If you disturb them in the spring, then flowering will at best be erratic. By lifting and dividing irises immediately flowering is over, they become well-established for the following season and produce a reasonable show. Do not be afraid to cut the foliage back hard. Separate clumps into individual fans of leaves and trim the roots back sharply before replanting them.

Feeding plants

Not all plants will require lifting, dividing and replanting, but the majority will certainly benefit from feeding. There are two methods of providing fertilizer for established plants without polluting the water. The traditional method is to mix clay and coarse bonemeal into 'bonemeal pills' that are thrust into the soil next to the plant. Each pill is made by mixing a handful of coarse bonemeal with sufficient wet clay to bind it together. It is a very practical way of introducing a slow-release fertilizer into an aquatic environment without polluting the water, the only question being how quickly the nutrients will be available to the plants. Recent research suggests that bonemeal takes much longer to release plant foods than had previously been thought.

The modern method, which is very straightforward and easy to administer, is to introduce specially manufactured aquatic fertilizer tablets or sachets of slow-release fertilizer to the planted baskets according to the manufacturers' recommendations. The sachets usually consist of a small package with a perforated section through which the fertilizer is slowly released.

Below: Be sure to use fertilizer tables that are specially formulated for aquatic plants. Push the tablet into the soil next to the plants. It will slowly release nutrients without polluting the water.

PROPAGATING POND PLANTS

The successful propagation of pond plants is within the capability of most home gardeners. Whether from seed, cuttings, eyes or winter buds, the majority of aquatic plants are easy to increase with the minimum of facilities.

Most aquatic plants are easy to propagate, although with seed-raised plants the condition of the seeds at both harvest time and after any storage determines success, rather than anything the competent gardener may do to help. Almost without exception, aquatic and bog garden plants germinate more freely from seed that is freshly gathered and sown immediately. Some, such as waterlily and water hawthorn (*Aponogeton distachyos*), perish if allowed to dry out, even if only for a few hours.

Choosing the right method

Division is the only reliable method of propagating variegated aquatic irises. Always use young, vigorous fans of foliage for reliable results.

Preparing seed-sowing medium
Sow seeds into a soil-based medium that has been shaken through a large, coarse sieve. Once thoroughly riddled in this way and then soaked with water, it should settle into a muddy consistency that is still a growing medium with a physical structure, rather than sticky mud. It should also

be devoid of – or very low in – nutrients, especially those that may dissolve into the water. Seedling waterlilies and marginal aquatics are very vulnerable to becoming smothered in algae, particularly the fine, soft silkweed kind, which is extremely difficult to remove from seedlings without causing damage.

Medium for cuttings

Most cuttings require a similar kind of medium, particularly those that grow right in the water. A muddy consistency is ideal for all manner of short-stem cuttings, from *Veronica beccabunga* and *Mentha aquatica* to *Mimulus ringens* (see page 63). However, those plants more properly referred to as bog plants, including lythrums, lysimachias and perennial lobelias, need a more conventional growing medium of equal parts peat and sand or something similar to root satisfactorily. Root cuttings also require a more conventional growing medium. Soil-based mediums are preferable to multipurpose types, as sticky mud and very wet mixtures are totally unsuitable and lead to rotting.

Taking cuttings and dividing plants

Always take cuttings of vigorous young shoots and make divisions from the outer portions of plants. The key to successful vegetative propagation is using healthy, youthful material. Discard the centre portions of mature plants, even normally vigorous ones, such as waterlilies. They take much longer to re-establish and often do not turn into well-balanced specimens.

With cuttings, it is vital to select strong, vigorous growth that is typical of the variety. Some plants have developed from mutations and it is possible to produce an inferior specimen if you do not use wholly characteristic foliage. This applies particularly to striped and variegated plants, which can be notoriously unstable and produce plain shoots.

Preparing cuttings

When preparing cuttings, try to produce a well-balanced shoot, with sufficient leaves to sustain life, but not so many that they transpire quicker than the cut stem can take up water. This rapidly leads to desiccation. For successful rooting, cut the base of the stem at a leaf joint. This is because all broad-leaved aquatics and bog garden plants that can be rooted from cuttings produce the cells that will initiate roots in greater numbers at a leaf joint.

Shading plants

Most aquatic plants benefit from wet conditions during propagation and there is normally little chance of them drying out. However, they should be partially shaded if they are to grow away strongly. Fine, green shade netting is ideal for young propagated plants, but a piece of newspaper, carefully secured over the pan or tray, is perfectly adequate for emerging seedlings. Although the majority of established aquatic plants enjoy full sun, as seedlings or cuttings they are vulnerable to leaf scorch, especially when growing on a window ledge or in a greenhouse.

Propagating waterlilies

There are three methods of increasing waterlilies: they can be propagated by division and from eyes and seed. Most pond owners opt for division. Even if you have no particular desire to increase their numbers, waterlilies must be regularly divided and replanted in order to prosper. Most of the popular varieties need dividing every three or four years.

Division

Spring is the ideal time to divide hardy waterlilies. Lift and wash each plant and remove any adult foliage. You will see that each plant consists of a main rootstock from which several eyes, or shoots, have grown to form sizable branches. It is these side growths that should be retained; simply cut them from the parent plant with as much rootstock as possible. The thick, bulky part of the original plant is generally of little use and should be discarded, but all the branches can be planted to form new plants as long as each one has a healthy terminal shoot.

Waterlilies from eyes

The majority of waterlilies can also be increased in the spring from eyes. These are tiny growing points that occur with varying frequency along the rootstocks of mature hardy

Dividing waterlilies

1 Wash the plant to remove all soil or growing medium. Identify individual crowns with strong growing points and separate them with a sharp knife.

2 Remove the bulk of the fibrous root growth and all superfluous foliage from each crown. Buoyant floating leaves may lift the plant out of the water.

3 Fill a large basket with aquatic planting medium or good clean garden soil and make a hole for the waterlily division. Plant the crown very firmly, with just the nose and any emerging leaves above soil level.

4 Once planted, it is important to soak the container thoroughly with water from a watering can with a fine rose. This drives all the air out of the planting medium and prevents disturbance when the basket is placed in the pool.

5 Cover the surface of the soil with a generous layer of pea gravel. This prevents the soil escaping into the water once the basket is submerged and also precludes fish from stirring it up in their quest for aquatic insect life.

6 Once again, thoroughly water the container to drive out any remaining air. This also washes any soil and organic debris from the gravel, which may escape and pollute the water once the waterlily is introduced to the pool.

waterlilies. They look like small versions of the main growing point, each with their cluster of leaves. However, with a few varieties, especially those derived from *Nymphaea tuberosa*, they appear as brittle rounded nodules that are easy to detach from the main plant.

Remove the eyes with a sharp knife and dust the exposed tissue of both eyes and rootstock with powdered charcoal. Pot individual eyes into containers of aquatic planting medium or good-quality, clean, heavy loam and stand them in a shallow container filled with sufficient water to cover the rims of the pots. As the young shoots develop, raise the water level and move the plants into successively larger pots until they are big enough to install in a large planting basket.

Waterlilies from seed

Some of the very fine hybrid waterlilies sometimes set seed and you can raise plants from this, but the chances are that they will not resemble the parents and in most cases will be inferior. Named varieties of waterlilies only come true from division or eyes. However, the tiny *Nymphaea tetragona* and N. 'Pygmaea Alba' can only be increased from seed, as they do not produce eyes or divide readily.

Seed is normally acquired from a fruiting plant and you must keep it

Propagating waterlilies from eyes

1 Remove the eyes or small shoots from the main rootstock with a sharp knife. Be sure to remove part of the starchy rootstock with the shoot.

2 Trim each eye of superfluous roots or debris. Wash thoroughly. If the cut surface looks vulnerable to infection, dust the wound with powdered charcoal.

constantly wet, from harvesting to sowing. When the fruits are ripe, they rupture and produce a clear gelatinous substance containing the seeds. Be sure to sow this sticky jelly with the seeds.

Use an aquatic planting medium or finely sieved heavy soil in a half-pot or pan and spread the jelly containing the seeds over the surface of the medium. Cover it lightly and then settle the soil by gently sprinkling it with water from a watering can fitted with a fine rose. Place the pan in a bowl or fish tank so that it is just submerged in clean water and stand it in a warm, light position. After three or four weeks the seedlings will appear. Once they are large enough to handle, prick them out into seed trays and place these in water. During their formative life, until they are large enough to pot up individually, watch the seedlings carefully for incursions of filamentous algae. Remove this gently so that it does not choke the young plantlets.

Raising aquatic plants from seed

Raising seed is one of the easiest methods of propagating both aquatic and bog plants, but remember that it is only the species that generally come true. However, amongst bog garden plants there are several named coloured strains of primulas and irises that are also raised in this way.

3 Place each eye into an individual small pot of aquatic planting medium. Firm in well, leaving just the tip of the shoot above the soil surface. Water thoroughly.

4 Place each pot into a bowl of tap water, making sure that the surface of the medium is completely submerged. As the leaves develop, add more water.

It is certainly the most satisfactory method of producing quantities of plants quickly and economically.

Marginals and aquatics from seed

Almost without exception, marginal and aquatic plants should be sown when the seed is fresh and still greenish. In some species, such as the water hawthorn (*Aponogeton distachyos)*, the seed must not only be slightly under-ripe, but also kept wet. Indeed, if it is allowed to leave the water before sowing it will perish within a few hours.

Sowing and raising the seeds

Sow the seeds of true aquatics in a wet, heavy loam and soak it thoroughly. In the case of plants with floating leaves, cover the planting medium with a shallow layer of

Below: The seeds of the majority of aquatic plants germinate more readily when sown directly after harvesting. Fresh iris seeds should emerge within three to four weeks of sowing.

water. Ideally, sow the seeds in plastic pots or pans of medium and use a small plastic aquarium as a plant nursery. When sowing seeds, be sure to cover them with soil and a thin layer of silver sand. This prevents them from floating away and the silver sand acts as a deterrent to algae invading the surface of the growing medium. Once the seeds have germinated and the seedlings are established, prick them out and treat them as recommended for young waterlily plants (see page 59).

Bog garden plants from seed

Bog garden plants are treated in a similar way, although the soil conditions should be damp rather than wet. Some gardeners raise bog plants in nursery beds in the open, but this is ill-advised, as the seeds are often very fine, the soil conditions lumpy and hostile, and watering difficult to control. Raising plants in pans or seed trays with the protection of a cold frame is much more satisfactory and the whole growing process is easier to manage.

Sowing bog garden plant seeds

The seeds of most bog garden plants are best sown fresh, which is all very well if you have access to fruiting plants, but can create problems if you depend on commercial seed suppliers. Collected seeds are usually sown during mid- to late summer shortly after gathering, whereas packeted seed rarely becomes available until winter or early spring. In some cases, particularly with bog garden primulas, seeds that are not

Left: You can sow seeds of aquatic plants directly onto the surface of aquatic soil in a shallow container. Keep the soil moist and put the container near a window for a few weeks. These seeds of sisyrinchium will sprout easily and the seedlings can be potted on into damp soil.

fresh must be chilled in order to break their dormancy.

Sow the seed in a good-quality soilless mixture and treat it as if it were fresh. Water it thoroughly and then place the seed pans or trays in the freezer, allowing them to remain there for a couple of weeks before returning them to the light and warmth. Germination usually follows quite rapidly. Once the seeds of bog garden plants have germinated, prick out the seedlings. When they have become established, transfer them carefully to individual pots and grow them on until they are large enough to be planted in their permanent positions. They usually reach this stage during the following spring.

Raising aquatic plants from cuttings

A number of marginal aquatic plants, most totally submerged plants and a sprinkling of bog garden subjects are increased by stem cuttings during

spring and summer. These are short pieces of healthy, ideally non-flowering stem taken from recent growth. Stem cuttings from marginal plants such as water mint *(Mentha aquatica)* and brooklime *(Veronica beccabunga)* are usually taken from overwintered parent plants in spring once the shoots are in active growth. With such plants, it is better to take the cuttings as early as possible in the season so that they can replace the

Above: Sisyrinchiums flourish at the edge of the pond in damp soil and will grow easily from seed sown in containers.

61

parent plants. Elderly water mint and brooklime rarely prosper in the same way as vigorous, freshly rooted cuttings. The best strategy is to treat them more or less as annuals.

Taking stem cuttings of marginals

Remove shoots up to 5cm (2in) long, cutting at a leaf joint. It is in the area of the leaf joint that the cells that will be stimulated into producing roots will be most active. Remove the lower leaves to prevent them from decomposing in the water. It is not usually necessary to use a hormone rooting preparation, as the majority of aquatic plants root very quickly in very wet planting medium or mud.

Place pans or trays containing the cuttings in a container of water. The water should just cover the surface of the soil. Shade the cuttings from direct sunlight; they should root within ten to fourteen days. Pot them on individually and allow them to produce small tight rootballs before grouping several together in an aquatic planting basket. If the cuttings start to grow vigorously without branching, pinch out the tips to encourage the development of bushy growth. If you remove the tips carefully, they can be rooted as cuttings, too.

Stem cuttings of submerged plants

With the exception of hairgrass (*Eleocharis acicularis*), which is increased by division, all the other popular submerged aquatics are increased by stem cuttings. The majority establish best if they are increased from vigorous young

growths early in the season, rather than older, brittle ones later on.

Remove good, strong healthy stems of non-flowering shoots. Clean up the foliage and gather together 5-10cm (2-4in)-long stems in small bunches. Fasten them neatly around the base with a thin strip of lead. This not only holds the bunches of cuttings together, but also weighs them down, which is an advantage when they are planted in their permanent container.

Plant the bunches of cuttings in aquatic planting baskets filled with

Below: When selecting cutting material, choose fresh healthy stems along which there is plenty of non-flowering lateral growth. This is best done between late spring and midsummer.

Taking cuttings of Mimulus ringens

Strip off flowers before using these shoots for cuttings.

Insert the cuttings in a pot of thoroughly soaked aquatic soil.

These are the ideal size for cuttings.

Arrange four cuttings around the edge of a 7.5cm (3in) plastic pot.

Above: *Taking cuttings from aquatic plants can be easier and more reliable than terrestrial plants. Follow these steps and keep the cuttings moist.*

Select fresh young vegetative shoots and prepare short cuttings. Remove the lower leaves, trimming back the upper foliage if necessary.

Increasing butomus from turions

1 Increase butomus by removing the turions that develop along the rootstock in late summer. Carefully lift the complete plant and wash the rootstock to expose the clusters of turions.

2 This mature butomus has a strong, creeping rootstock and dense clusters of turions. Some of those from the previous year are developing into new plants; you can separate them now.

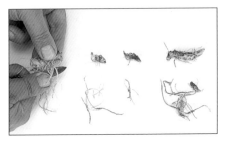

3 Carefully remove the tiny turions from the rootstock, each with a vestige of root attached. If necessary, cut them off with a sharp knife. Separate and pot up larger growths individually.

4 Trim back the roots and place three or four turions into a small pot of aquatic planting medium. Firm them in gently. Grow them on until sufficiently large to separate and pot individually. Stand the freshly potted turions in a container of tap water that just covers the rim of the pots. Regularly remove any algae that appear, especially the coarse filamentous blanketweed kinds.

a good-quality aquatic plant medium or heavy loam or clay soil. Bury the lead weight beneath the medium, otherwise it will rot through the stems and the top portion of the cuttings will float away. Topdress the baskets with pea gravel, water them thoroughly and place them directly into the pond.

Bog plants from root cuttings
Amongst the bog garden plants are some that can be increased by root cuttings, notably the candelabra and drumstick primulas. Take root cuttings during the dormant season by lifting the parent plant and removing short cuttings of healthy root up to 2.5cm (1in) long. Place them horizontally in seed trays of good-quality seed mixture, lightly cover them with more mixture, water them and place them in a cold frame. When the pieces of root start to sprout in spring, lift and pot them up individually for growing on ready for planting later the following year.

Raising plants from turions
A number of aquatic plants produce winter storage organs, or turions. In some cases, as with the arrowhead (Sagittaria sagittifolia) or flowering rush (Butomus umbellatus), these are primarily food storage organs. However, they are freely produced and, with careful separation, can become individual plants. If left to their own devices, they form sizable, solid clumps that in due course will have to be lifted and separated if the plants are to continue to develop satisfactorily.

Some submerged plants and a number of floating aquatics produce winter turions in a clear effort to multiply. This especially applies to the frogbit (Hydrocharis morsus-ranae), which breaks up into a dozen or more individual plantlets as autumn approaches. At first, these are attached by runners, but eventually they turn into hard, fat, leafless buds that sink to the floor of the pool to overwinter.

The water soldier (Stratiotes aloides) behaves in a similar way, but usually retains an old brittle plant around which are clustered tiny plantlets, each attached by a runner rather like the indoor spider plant. In due course these either separate, or in the spring they can be divided and redistributed.

The hornwort (Ceratophyllum demersum) all but disappears for the winter, its bristly stems receding until only a tight bud remains. These quite naturally divide and redistribute without any intervention by the water gardener.

Raising aquatic plants by division
Most marginal plants and all waterlilies and other deep water aquatics require regular division in order to flourish. How often you have to divide them depends on the variety, but it is usually every two or three years or, in the case of waterlilies, four or sometimes five years. Where you are dividing plants with the aim of improving the established planting, retain the youngest, most vigorous portions of the plants and discard the older

material. The same applies when your intention is to increase the stock of plants. Always use the youngest material first, although you can select, separate and use any live material. It is just that it may not establish and grow away as strongly.

What is division?

For the majority of plants, division is simply the process by which a crown is divided into sustainable portions that are potted or planted out individually. In the case of plants such as reedmaces and rushes, which have creeping root systems, this often involves removing lengths of rootstock, each with a terminal bud, trimming these up and potting them individually. Effectively, each division is a large bud or shoot with a small cluster of roots.

When to divide?

The majority of aquatic and bog garden plants are divided in the early spring, just as their shoots are emerging. Plants that flower at this time, such as marsh marigolds and the early drumstick primulas, are best dealt with as soon as their blossoms have faded. Astilbes, hostas and other popular bog garden plants are sometimes split up during the depths of winter. Although this is perfectly satisfactory, it is often not as easy to do as in early spring, especially with hostas. In the autumn or winter it is often necessary to use a knife when dealing with established clumps, while in the spring, once the plants have started into growth, you can just pull them apart.

Dividing irises

Above: Lift established clumps of irises carefully. Ideally, do this immediately after flowering so that the divisions become established before the following season, although division can be undertaken all summer long.

Above: Thoroughly wash the clump and separate out individual fans of leaves. These should pull apart quite easily. Select the younger, more vigorous individuals for replanting.

Shorten the leaves with a sharp knife.

Plant the divisions singly into small mesh containers filled with aquatic planting mix or heavy garden soil.

Divide the clump into separate fans of leaves, such as these.

Reduce the length of the roots.

Left: Position the basket carefully on the marginal shelf, initially in water that just comes over the top of the basket. If the water is deeper, prop the basket up on a brick until it has become established and then lower it gently.

67

PESTS AND DISEASES

Pond plants are subject to a variety of pests and diseases.
Most are disfiguring rather than debilitating and are readily
controlled by good husbandry and pond hygiene rather
than garden chemicals, which are harmful to fish.

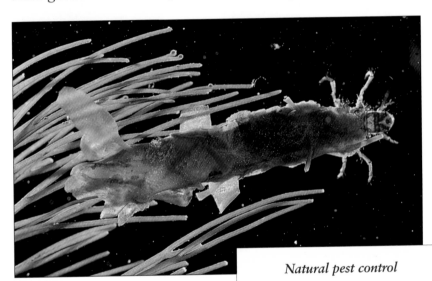

As with all garden plants, those that inhabit the water garden are subject to a range of pests that can cause disfigurement and occasionally death. They can be particularly troublesome if fish are living in the pool, because it is difficult to use insecticides without putting the fish at risk. So the life cycle of each pest has to be carefully observed in order to destroy it when it is at its most vulnerable.

Waterlily aphids
The best example of this is the waterlily aphid, probably the most

common of all the afflictions of aquatic plants. The aphids breed at a prodigious rate during warm humid weather and attack the flowers and foliage of waterlilies and other succulent aquatics with impunity. Indeed, they have the same kind of effect upon aquatic plants as black bean aphids have on broad beans.

Above: Waterlily aphids feed on all succulent pond plants. Applying a winter wash to nearby plum and cherry trees kills the overwintering generation and breaks the life cycle of these pests.

They are a major disfiguring pest. Eggs from the late summer brood of adults are laid on plum and cherry trees during early autumn, where they overwinter. These hatch in the spring and winged female adults fly to the water plants, where they reproduce asexually every few days. As autumn approaches, a winged generation is produced, which flies to the trees and deposits eggs.

During the summer, spraying the foliage regularly with a strong jet of clear water is the only way of controlling the pests. As they are knocked into the water, they are cleared up by the fish. Insecticides are not much use unless the pond is free from fish. However, much can be done during the winter to break the life cycle of the aphids by spraying nearby plum and cherry trees with a winter wash. This destroys the overwintering eggs.

Waterlily beetles
Waterlily beetles can be equally irritating and are a very tiresome pest to control. The leaves of waterlilies become stripped of their surface layer by the distinctive black, yellow-bellied larvae, and then begin to rot. The small dark brown beetles hibernate in poolside vegetation during the winter and migrate to the waterlilies during early summer,

Above: Most gardeners regard dragonflies as a welcome addition to the pool, although fish lovers are not enthusiastic about them laying eggs in waterside vegetation, as these turn into voracious larvae that delight in preying on small fish.

where they deposit their eggs on the leaf surfaces. After a week or so, the larvae hatch out and begin their destruction. There can be several broods in a season.

The only practical control method is to hose down the leaves regularly in order to dislodge the pests so that they can be devoured by the fish. Taking great care to remove any marginal plant foliage during the winter reduces the opportunity for overwintering beetles to hide up in close proximity to the pool. Once waterlily beetles become well

established in an area, constant vigilance will be required to prevent them from devastating the plants.

False leaf-mining midge
False leaf-mining midge can produce superficially similar symptoms to waterlily beetle, because the larvae of this tiny creature eat a narrow tracery of lines over the surface of the foliage of floating-leaved aquatics. The damaged areas start to decay and the leaves becomes detached and start to decompose. Rarely is damage as extensive as that caused by waterlily beetles, but it can be very disfiguring. There is no cure except the regular forcible spraying of floating foliage with a clear jet of water, although occasionally in severe cases the floating leaves are best removed and destroyed. The new emerging foliage will then often escape predation.

Caddis flies
Caddis flies are an interesting pest, because although their larvae can cause considerable damage, most pond owners have a grudging admiration for the way in which they use the foliage that they remove from pond plants in the construction of their shelters. The majority of caddis flies are totally aquatic in their larval stage and swim around inside little shelters made from sticks, sand, shells and pieces of plant.

The adult flies visit the pool in the evening, depositing eggs in a mass of jelly, which swells up immediately it touches the water. This will often be hooked around submerged foliage or attached to a marginal plant so that it trails into the water. When the eggs hatch out, the larvae immediately start to spin their silky cases, collecting all manner of pond and plant debris. At the same time they feed freely on any aquatic plants. Eventually, they pupate in the pool or amongst marginal plants around the edge. Specific spraying or hand picking controls are impossible. Generally speaking, caddis fly larvae are a pest that pondkeepers learn to live with; they can be kept to a tolerable level by the activities of fish.

Brown china mark moth
The brown china mark moth larvae also take pieces out of the foliage of aquatic plants and provide a shelter for themselves prior to pupation by sticking down leaf fragments in which to weave a greyish silky cocoon. The damage is sometimes

extensive; plants have torn and distorted leaves that are subject to fungal attack and then start to crumble around the edges.

During late summer, the eggs of this insignificant moth are laid in neat rows on the foliage of any floating-leaved pond plant. The eggs quickly hatch and tiny caterpillars emerge and burrow into the undersides of the succulent foliage, eventually making small oval cases out of these leaves. During the winter they hibernate, re-emerging in the spring to continue their trails of destruction across the pond.

Small infestations can be picked off by hand. Net off all pieces of floating foliage and discard them in

Below: The greater pond snail will feed on algae, but much prefers to graze on succulent aquatic plants causing considerable damage.

case they have cocoons attached. When damage is widespread, cut off all the floating foliage and remove it. This enables the plants to have a fresh start. Regeneration is usually quite rapid.

China mark moth
The beautiful china mark moth can also be very destructive, but occurs far less frequently. The adult moth resembles its cousin in appearance and in its life cycle, except that instead of initially destroying the foliage of floating-leaved aquatics, the larvae of this pest burrow into the stems of the plants, where they eventually hibernate. Later they emerge to make leaf cases and ultimately their white silky cocoons. There is no control other than to pick them off by hand.

Pond snails
Pond snails can be a really tiresome pest, especially the greater pond snail. Unfortunately, it is often introduced to a pool in the mistaken belief that it will feed on algae. It may occasionally graze on blanketweed, but it much prefers the soft, succulent, floating foliage of waterlilies. Generally speaking, you should avoid pointed-shelled aquatic snails, as most will feed on pond plants. The only safe snails to introduce are the planorbis, or ramshorn snails, which have flat, disclike shells.

Picking undesirable snails out by hand is the only reliable method of controlling them in the pond, but you can aid the process by floating a fresh lettuce leaf on the water overnight. The snails congregate beneath it and are easy to remove and discard the following morning.

Diseases
Fortunately, there are few diseases that attack aquatic plants, and with the exception of waterlily crown rot, they are fairly innocuous. The two common waterlily leaf spots are disfiguring, but rarely if ever cause the demise of the plants they attack.

Waterlily leaf spots
One form of waterlily leaf spot causes dark patches to appear on the surface of floating foliage. These eventually rot through and in severe cases the leaves disintegrate. The other form starts along the edge of the leaves, causing them to turn brown and crumble. There is no set pattern for attack; in some years the problem is persistent, while in others it does not appear at all. This seems to be related to the weather conditions, especially temperature.

Waterlily crown rot
Waterlily crown rot can be devastating. There appear to be two distinct kinds, one of which has been around for many years and is universally blamed on phytophthora, a fungus related to the blight of potatoes and tomatoes. This tends to be prevalent among yellow-flowered waterlilies, although it does attack other colours, too. The symptoms of this particular crown rot are a blackening of the leaves and flower stems, which become soft and rotten,

the rootstocks turning foul smelling, pinkish and gelatinous.

Remove and destroy affected crowns, remove the fish and clean out the pool thoroughly. Fill a muslin bag with copper sulphate crystals and swirl it vigorously through the water as a disinfection before final draining. Then reintroduce fresh clean water and replant the pond.

The more virulent and deadly form of waterlily crown rot has caused serious problems in recent years and is little understood. It is believed to have been imported on waterlily crowns from the Far East and attacks all waterlilies, irrespective of variety, causing the crowns to collapse into a decomposing brown mass. As there is little understanding of the precise cause of this particular rot, it is difficult to recommend a strategy for its control, although at present commercial growers recommend cleaning out the pool thoroughly and sterilising it with a solution of sodium hypochlorite before flushing it out with fresh clean water.

Mildew

Occasionally, marginal aquatics, especially marsh marigolds or calthas, suffer from mildew. This is a greyish mould that attacks the foliage, usually long after flowering. It is ugly rather than debilitating and in most cases is best dealt with by cutting off infected foliage. If the mildew is causing real problems for the plant, as sometimes happens with the white flowered *Caltha palustris* var. *alba*, and it is established in a

container, then remove it from the pond in its container and spray it with a systemic fungicide.

Systemic fungicides

Modern systemic chemical treatments are inactivated when they reach the soil or growing medium and once they have dried on the foliage present no problems for fish or other aquatic creatures when the plants are reintroduced to the pond. Systemic fungicides work by being absorbed through the foliage of the plant and circulating through the sap stream, effectively inoculating the plant against attack. Such treatment will often be necessary a second time.

Above: *Mildew often attacks marsh marigolds towards the end of the growing season. It is disfiguring rather than debilitating and is best dealt with by cutting off the affected foliage. A systemic fungicide can be used in severe cases.*

PART TWO

A selection of pond plants

A well-planted pond, created with a practical balance in mind, is usually aesthetically pleasing because it embraces all classes of pond plant in moderate quantities with sufficient open water to add to their appeal. Then, by selecting specific plants within the categories desired, you can begin to paint a horticultural picture. Most aquatic plants are simple to grow, but they offer tremendous diversity and in order to produce an attractive and easily maintained water garden feature it is essential to learn something of their behaviour before introducing them to the pond.

In addition to creating a floral picture, plants make a major contribution to wildlife, whether this is intended or not. Many native and introduced aquatic plants, especially among the marginals, have an important role to play in the life cycle of butterflies and other insects. Beneath the water, the trailing roots of floating plants and the fine, fernlike, congested foliage of submerged aquatics provide living quarters for aquatic insect life and a haven for spawning fish and emerging fry.

Pond plants are the mainstay of a water feature and in addition to all their practical benefits and aesthetic values, they have an individual fascination. No other part of the plant kingdom offers such a rich diversity of habit, character and colour. This part of the book features a selection of pond plants, from waterlilies and marginals to submerged, floating and bog garden subjects. The text entries describe the plants and how to grow and propagate them, and the essence of many is captured in attractive artwork illustrations.

WATERLILIES

Waterlilies are the queens of the water garden – beautiful, exotic and colourful aquatics that provide a wonderful summer-long display. There are varieties for all occasions and situations, from the smallest tub to the largest lake, for the formal water garden as well as the wildlife pool. Here is a selection of some of the most popular varieties.

PYGMY WATERLILIES

Nymphaea 'Pygmaea Alba'
● Pygmy white waterlily

Depth: 10-30cm (4-12in)
Spread: 20-40cm (8-16in)
Description: A perfect miniature waterlily for growing in a tub or sink, or in the margins of a large pool. Tiny, papery, white flowers no more than 2.5cm (1in) across are produced amongst small, roughly oval dark green leaves with purple undersides.
Propagation: This is the only hardy waterlily that can be successfully raised from seed. Sow the seeds in trays of heavy, soil-based potting mixture as soon as they ripen and place the trays in a bowl or aquarium.

Nymphaea 'Pygmaea Helvola'

Depth: 10-30cm (4-12in)
Spread: 20-60cm (8-24in)
Description: This is the easiest and most free-flowering of the pygmy waterlilies. Beautiful canary-yellow blossoms with bright orange stamens are produced amongst olive-green leaves that are heavily splashed and stained with purple and brown.
Propagation: Divide established crowns during the growing season or remove young eyes.

Right: Nymphaea *'Pygmaea Helvola' is the most popular of the charming pygmy waterlilies. As with all the miniature varieties, it is best grown in a tub or container, rather than in the garden pond.*

PYGMY WATERLILIES

N. 'Pygmaea Alba'
(left) is the tiniest
of all the
waterlilies. Best
grown in a tub or
large container.

N. 'Pygmaea Helvola'
(right) is very free-
flowering and ideal
for a container water
garden or the
marginal shelf.

N. 'Pygmaea
Rubra' (left) is a
fine water lily for
the container water
garden, although it
takes a season to
become fully
established.

Nymphaea 'Pygmaea Rubra'

Depth: 10-30cm (4-12in)
Spread: 20-60cm (8-24in)
Description: Tiny blood-red blossoms with orange-red stamens are produced amongst purplish-green leaves with distinctive reddish undersides. It is an ideal waterlily for a tub garden or the margins of a larger pool.
Propagation: Remove young eyes from the rootstock and pot them individually in a heavy, soil-based potting mix. This variety rarely divides successfully.

SMALL WATERLILIES

Nymphaea 'Aurora'

Depth: 30-45cm (12-18in)
Spread: 30-60cm (12-24in)
Description: A reliable waterlily with attractive purplish-and-green mottled leaves and blossoms that change colour with each passing day. In this chameleon, or changeable, waterlily, the blossoms start off cream in bud, opening to a yellow flower that then passes through orange shades to blood red.
Propagation: Divide established crowns during the growing season or remove young eyes.

Nymphaea 'Graziella'

Depth: 30-60cm (12-24in)
Spread: 30-75cm (12-30in)
Description: Orange-red flowers, scarcely more than 5cm (2in) in diameter and with deep orange stamens, are freely produced throughout the summer. The

olive-green leaves are liberally blotched with brown and purple.
Propagation: Divide established crowns during the growing season or remove young eyes.

Nymphaea 'Laydekeri Purpurata'

Depth: 30-60cm (12-24in)
Spread: 45-75cm (18-30cm)
Description: A small-growing waterlily with rich vinous-red flowers and bright orange stamens. The leaves are small and dark green but purple beneath and often marked on the surface with black or maroon splashes.
Propagation: Divide established crowns during the growing season or remove young eyes.

Above: Any waterlily belonging to the Laydekeri group is suitable for the smaller pool. Nymphaea 'Laydekeri Purpurata' is the most free-flowering and easiest variety to grow.

SMALL WATERLILIES

N. *'Aurora'*
*(right) is one of the
changeable, or chameleon,
waterlilies, with flowers
that start cream in bud
and pass through
yellow and orange to
red with each
passing day.*

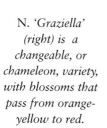

N. *'Laydekeri
Purpurata' (left) is the
most free-flowering,
small-growing red
variety, with a sweet
fragrance.*

N. *'Graziella'
(right) is a
changeable, or
chameleon, variety,
with blossoms that
pass from orange-
yellow to red.*

MEDIUM-GROWING WATERLILIES

Nymphaea 'Albatros'

Depth: 30-60cm (12-24in)
Spread: 60-120cm (24-48in)
Description: One of the finest medium-growing waterlilies, with large, pure white blossoms and central clusters of bright yellow stamens. The leaves are rounded and purplish when young, but deep green when fully expanded.
Propagation: Divide established crowns during the growing season or remove young eyes.

Above: Nymphaea 'Froebeli' is an old, very hardy, and well tried variety, suitable for the small or medium-sized pool. Once well established, it will flower freely from late spring throughout the summer and into early autumn.

Nymphaea 'Arc-en-ciel'

Depth: 60-90cm (24-36in)
Spread: 90-120cm (36-48in)
Description: This variety is grown for its beautiful variegated foliage, rather than for the soft, blush-pink, papery flowers that only appear occasionally. The olive-green leaves are splashed and stained with purple, rose, white and bronze.
Propagation: Divide established crowns during the growing season or remove young eyes.

Nymphaea 'Froebeli'

Depth: 45-60cm (18-24in)
Spread: 45-75cm (18-30in)
Description: One of the most popular free-flowering waterlilies for the smaller pool. Deep blood-red blossoms with orange stamens are produced amongst purplish-green leaves. Once established, it is one of the finest red waterlilies.
Propagation: Divide established crowns during the growing season or remove young eyes.

Nymphaea 'Gonnère'

Depth: 45-75cm (18-30in)
Spread: 75-90cm (30-36in)
Description: A most exceptional waterlily, with multipetalled, globular blossoms of the purest white that look rather like floating snowballs. It also has conspicuous pea-green stamens and very attractive rounded, bright green leaves.
Propagation: Divide established crowns during the growing season or remove young eyes.

Left: Of all the yellow flowered waterlilies, Nymphaea *'Marliacea Chromatella'* provides the best display. Not only does it have beautifully sculptured blossoms, but it also sports handsome, olive green leaves, boldly splashed with maroon and bronze.

Nymphaea 'Marliacea Albida'

Depth: 45-90cm (18-36in)
Spread: 75-120cm (30-48in)
Description: A popular and very easily grown free-flowering waterlily, with large pure white, fragrant blooms held just out of the water. The stamens are yellow and the sepals and backs of the petals are often flushed with soft pink. The large deep green leaves have red or purplish undersides.
Propagation: Divide established crowns during the growing season or remove young eyes.

Nymphaea 'Marliacea Chromatella'

Depth: 45-75cm (18-30in)
Spread: 90-120cm (36-48in)
Description: This is the most popular yellow-flowered waterlily. It has slightly fragrant blossoms up to 15cm (6in) in diameter, with broad, incurved canary yellow petals surrounding a central boss of deep golden-yellow stamens. The pale yellow sepals are flushed with pink. The handsome olive-green rounded leaves are boldly splashed with maroon and bronze.
Propagation: Divide established crowns during the growing season or remove young eyes.

Nymphaea 'Moorei'

Depth: 45-75cm (18-30in)
Spread: 75-90cm (30-36in)
Description: A beautiful soft-yellow-flowered waterlily, with pale green leaves distinctively and irregularly sprinkled with purple spots. The best yellow waterlily for the small to medium-sized pool. 'Moorei' is distinctive in having plain green flower and leaf stems, whereas those of the other varieties are striped with red.
Propagation: Divide established crowns during the growing season or remove young eyes.

MEDIUM-GROWING WATERLILIES

N. 'Moorei'
(left) is a fine, free-
flowering
Australian waterlily
for the medium-
sized pool.

N. 'Albatros'
(below) has
beautifully sculptured
blossoms and
handsome green
foliage that is purple
when young.

82

N. 'Froebeli' *(right)*
is *an excellent free-*
flowering and very
hardy variety for
the medium-
sized pool.

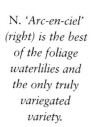

N. 'Gonnère'
(left) is the only
fully double-
flowered white
variety of
waterlily.

N. 'Arc-en-ciel'
(right) is the best
of the foliage
waterlilies and
the only truly
variegated
variety.

N. 'Marliacea Chromatella' (left) produces canary-yellow flowers amongst olive-green leaves that are splashed and marked with maroon brown.

N. 'Rose Arey' (right) holds its starry, sugar icing pink flowers just above handsome, fresh green leaves. The blooms have a strong aniseed fragrance.

N. 'Marliacea Albida' (left) is an old, but popular and reliable, white-flowered variety that prospers in most situations. It is the best white variety for a wildlife pool.

Nymphaea 'Rose Arey'

Depth: 45-75cm (18-30in)
Spread: 60-120cm (24-48in)
Description: A widely grown and much-loved waterlily, with large, open, starlike flowers, a central boss of golden stamens and an overpowering aniseed fragrance. The plain green leaves are tinged with red, the juvenile foliage being crimson until it breaks the surface of the water.
Propagation: Divide established crowns during the growing season or remove young eyes.

LARGE-GROWING WATERLILIES

Nymphaea 'Escarboucle'

Depth: 60-180cm (24-72in)
Spread: 90-270cm (36-106in)
Description: The finest red waterlily when given sufficient space to grow freely. The blossoms are deep crimson, fragrant and have a central boss of bright yellow stamens. The leaves are very large, rounded and plain green.
Propagation: Divide established crowns during the growing season or remove young eyes.

Nymphaea 'Gladstoneana'

Depth: 60-240cm (24-96in)
Spread: 120-300cm (48-118in)
Description: A vigorous-growing waterlily with very large, pure white blossoms. These are slightly fragrant and have a distinctive yellow, central cluster of stamens. The leaves are large, dark green and circular.
Propagation: Divide established crowns during the growing season or remove young eyes.

Nymphaea 'Marliacea Carnea'

Depth: 45-150cm (18-60in)
Spread: 75-180cm (30-72in)
Description: This waterlily produces large, flesh-pink blossoms with bright yellow stamens and a distinctive vanilla fragrance. Flowers on newly established plants are often white for the first season. The leaves are large, rounded and purplish when young, but deep green on maturity.
Propagation: Divide established crowns during the growing season or remove young eyes.

Above: *For the larger pool, few waterlilies surpass the lovely flesh pink-flowered* Nymphaea *'Marliacea Carnea' with its distinctive vanilla fragrance. An old and trusted variety for most situations.*

LARGE WATERLILIES

Nymphaea 'Marliacea Carnea' (right) has large flesh-pink blossoms with a vanilla fragrance above deep green leaves that are flushed with purple when young.

Nymphaea 'Gladstoneana' (left) freely produces enormous pure white flowers with conspicuous golden centres amongst dark green lily pads.

Nymphaea 'Escarboucle' (right) is the best large-flowered red variety. It has deep crimson, fragrant blossoms with contrasting bright yellow centres.

TROPICAL WATERLILIES

Right: N. 'Mrs George H. Pring' is one of the most popular day-blooming tropical waterlilies. Its very beautiful white, starry blossoms are fragrant and held well above the large reddish-brown daubed leaves. In temperate climates, grow tropical water-lilies in a warm green-house or conservatory.

Below: Amongst the night-flowering tropical waterlilies, the large, rose-pink 'Mrs George C. Hitchcock' is outstanding. It has a modest growth habit and will grow in a tub.

Deep water aquatics

Apart from waterlilies, there is a range of handsome aquatic plants that require deep water for their successful cultivation. These are mostly grown alongside the waterlilies in the central part of the pond.

Aponogeton distachyos
● Water hawthorn

Depth: 30-90cm (12-36in)
Description: A wonderful vanilla-scented plant, with forked blossoms that consist of two white bractlike organs with black stamens. The dark olive-green floating leaves, rectangular in outline but with rounded ends, are occasionally splashed with maroon or deep purple.
Propagation: Divide established plants during early spring. Easy to raise from seed if sown when fresh and green.

Nymphoides peltata
● Water fringe

Depth: 30-75cm (12-30in)
Description: A lovely aquatic, with heart-shaped, fresh green leaves occasionally blotched with brown or maroon. The leaves spread across the surface of the water. The flowers are dainty, bright yellow and attractively fringed. Suitable for both a decorative pool and a wildlife water garden.
Propagation: Easy to increase by separating out the runners and detaching them as individual plants, each with a portion of root.

Orontium aquaticum
● Golden club

Depth: 45cm (18in)
Description: During midsummer this curious plant produces bright gold-and-white pencil-like flower spikes that are held well above the surface of the water amongst floating masses of glaucous lanceshaped foliage.
Propagation: Immediately they ripen, sow fresh seeds in trays of mud.

*Above: The golden club (*Orontium aquaticum*) is a very hardy plant from North America. Once well established, this strange relative of the arum lily flowers reliably every year.*

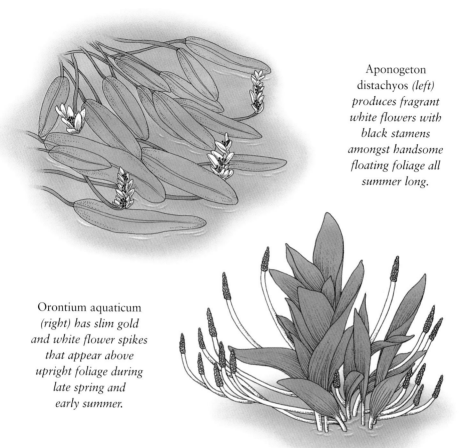

Aponogeton distachyos *(left) produces fragrant white flowers with black stamens amongst handsome floating foliage all summer long.*

Orontium aquaticum *(right) has slim gold and white flower spikes that appear above upright foliage during late spring and early summer.*

Nymphoides peltata *(left) has bright yellow blossoms carried just above masses of rounded floating foliage throughout the summer.*

89

MARGINAL PLANTS

'Marginals' is the word used to describe those plants that enjoy growing in the shallow waters at the poolside. Although they have little impact on the ecological balance of the pond, they provide much of the colour, variety and decorative interest from early spring until the autumn.

Acorus calamus 'Variegatus'
● Variegated sweet flag

Water depth: Moist soil to 5cm (2in)
Height: 90-120cm (36-48in)
Description: Green, cream and rose variegated foliage that looks rather like an iris. The long, swordlike leaves release a fragrance of tangerines if bruised. Insignificant, yellowish green spikelike flowers appear amongst the foliage during the summer.
Propagation: Divide the fleshy rhizomes during the active growing season.

Alisma plantago-aquatica
● Water plantain

Water depth: Moist soil to 15cm (6in)
Height: 60-90cm (24-36in)
Description: A plant with bright green oval leaves carried upright through the water and loose panicles of pink and white flowers. The old flowerheads become woody once blossoming is over and can be gathered or dried for indoor floral decoration.
Propagation: Immediately they ripen, sow seed in trays of mud or divide plants during the growing season.

Butomus umbellatus
● Flowering rush

Water depth: Moist soil to 23cm (9in)
Height: 60-90cm (24-36in)
Description: A handsome plant with irregular, angular, rushlike foliage. Spreading umbels of showy rose-pink flowers appear during mid- to late summer. Plant it in full sun.
Propagation: Remove bulbils from the base of mature plants or divide it during the growing season.

Calla palustris
● Bog arum

Water depth: Moist soil to 5cm (2in)
Height: 15-30cm (6-12in)
Description: The bog arum is an excellent scrambling plant for disguising the edge of the pool. Its strong creeping stems are

Right: The water plantain (Alisma plantago-aquatica) *is a valuable plant for both garden and wildlife pools. It seeds freely, so be sure to manage it carefully so that it does not become a nuisance.*

Alisma plantago-aquatica *(left) produces spreading panicles of white- or pink-flushed flowers from amongst broad, upright green leaves during summer.*

Acorus calamus 'Variegatus' *(below) has handsome swordlike cream-and-green variegated leaves that are strongly flushed with red in spring.*

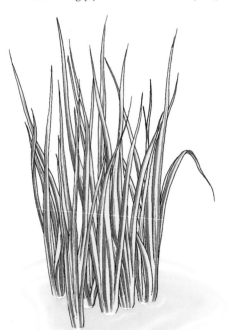

Butomus umbellatus *(above) produces umbels of bright rose-pink flowers from clumps of narrow, slightly twisted foliage during midsummer.*

Calla palustris
(right) has small, white sail-
like flowers that appear
among the glossy green
leaves during late spring
and early summer.

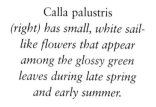

Caltha palustris
(below) is the earliest
pondside flowering plant.

Caltha palustris 'Flore Pleno'
(above) bears a profusion of
fully double, golden yellow
flowers above short, compact
clumps of dark green leaves
during spring .

Caltha palustris *var.* alba
(left) produces white
flowers with golden
centres on compact plants
with mounds of fresh
green leaves.

densely clothed with bright, glossy green, heart-shaped foliage. Small white blossoms, rather like those of the peace lily, are produced during late spring or early summer, followed by spikes of succulent orange-red fruits, which remain until autumn.

Propagation: Cut the creeping stems into small sections, each with a bud, and plant the pieces in trays of mud in spring or sow seed as soon as it ripens.

Caltha palustris
- Marsh marigold

Water depth: Moist soil to 30cm (12in)
Height: 30-60cm (12-24in)
Description: A handsome plant, with dark green mounds of scalloped foliage smothered with bright golden yellow, waxy flowers during early spring. A great asset for a pool early in the year, as there are few other aquatic plants in flower at this time.
Propagation: Divide during the growing season or sow seed in trays of mud immediately it ripens.

Caltha palustris var. alba

Water depth: Moist soil to 20cm (8in)
Height: 20-40cm (8-16in)
Description: A compact, early spring flowering marginal aquatic, with dark green rounded foliage and dense clusters of white waxy blossoms with yellow stamens. This variety often becomes disfigured by mildew towards the end of the year. Simply trim off affected foliage
Propagation: Divide during the growing season.

Caltha palustris 'Flore Pleno'
- Double marsh marigold

Water depth: Moist soil to 5cm (2in)
Height: 15-30cm (6-12in)
Description: An excellent spring-flowering aquatic for a smaller pool. Double, bright golden yellow blossoms, not unlike pompom chrysanthemums, are borne above bright green glossy foliage.
Propagation: Divide established plants during the growing season.

Cotula coronopifolia
- Brass buttons

Water depth: Moist soil to 5cm (2in)
Height: 15cm (6in)
Description: A truly aquatic relative of the popular rock garden cotulas, this plant produces masses of bright yellow buttonlike flowers above dense light green foliage throughout the summer. As it is a self-seeding annual, regular dead-heading is essential.
Propagation: Sow seed during early spring in trays in a cold frame.

Cyperus longus
- Sweet galingale

Water depth: Moist soil to 15cm (6in)
Height: 90-120cm (36-48in)
Description: A grassy plant, with fresh green, spiky leaves that radiate from the stems, rather like the ribs of an umbrella. Small brownish flowerheads are scattered amongst the upper leaves. This strong-growing plant has a creeping, matlike root system.

Propagation: Sow seed into trays of mud as soon as it ripens, or divide plants carefully during spring.

Eriophorum angustifolium
● Cotton grass

Water depth: Moist soil to 5cm (2in)
Height: 30-45cm (12-18in)
Description: A handsome plant, with fine grassy foliage and cottonwool-like flowerheads. It must have very acid conditions to succeed and is ideal when planted into a container filled with acid soil mixed with liberal quantities of peat.
Propagation: Divide established plants in spring. You can sow freshly gathered seed, but germination is irregular.

Glyceria maxima var. *variegata*
● Variegated water grass

Water depth: Moist soil to 30cm (12in)
Height: 60-120cm (24-48in)
Description: A vigorous aquatic grass that is equally happy growing in mud or relatively deep flowing water. The green-and-cream strongly variegated foliage has a strong, rose-pink tinge during early spring. Spikes of off-white flowerheads appear during the summer.
Propagation: Divide established plants during early spring.

Houttuynia cordata 'Chameleon'

Water depth: Moist soil to 5cm (2in)
Height: 15-30cm (6-12in)
Description: A creeping plant for the shallows of the pool, where it can be extremely useful for disguising a harsh or unpleasant edge. The strongly variegated red, yellow, cream and green heart-shaped leaves have an unpleasant smell when handled. The occasional flowers are creamy white, four-petalled and with a hard, conelike centre.
Propagation: Divide the creeping rootstocks in spring.

Left: Houttuynia cordata *'Chameleon' is one of the most colourful creeping plants for disguising the harsh edge of the artificial pond during the summer months. It dies back in winter.*

Houttuynia cordata
(right) is a reliable
purplish-green
foliage plant that
produces interesting
creamy-white
flowers with
conelike centres.

Eriophorum angustifolium
(left) has fluffy, white
flowerheads scattered
amongst clumps of dark
green grassy foliage.

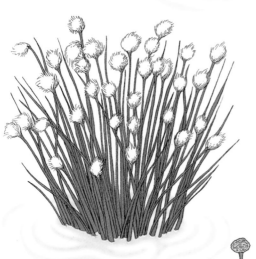

Cotula coronopifolia
(right) is a colourful
annual, with masses of
buttonlike yellow flowers
produced all summer long
amongst divided, mid-
green foliage.

Cyperus longus
*(right) has narrow, dark green,
grassy leaves with small
brownish flowers that arise from
a creeping, matlike rootstock.*

Glyceria maxima *var.* variegata
*(below) is a vigorous-growing
cream-and-green variegated
grass, with a strong rose-pink
flush early in the season.*

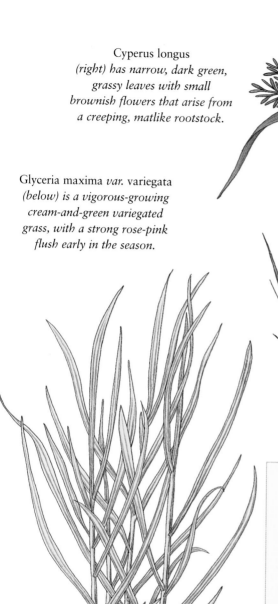

Cyperus alternifolius

The umbrella plant (*Cyperus
alternifolius*) is well-named, as
its spiky leaves radiate from the
stems like an umbrella. It is one
of the most versatile marginal
plants, as it will grow well in
both temperate and tropical
climates. However, it will not
overwinter outdoors where there
is a danger of frost. In such
circumstances, it can spend the
winter indoors as a pot plant.

Iris laevigata
● Asiatic water iris

Water depth: 5-10cm (2-4in)
Height: 50-90cm (20-36in)
Description: A clump-forming plant with smooth, sword-shaped leaves for full sun. The species has blue flowers during early and midsummer. Of the named varieties, 'Atropurpurea' is purple-blue, 'Rose Queen' is soft pink and 'Snowdrift' is white. All are widely grown.
Propagation: Divide established plants immediately after flowering. *Iris laevigata* can be raised from seed sown in trays of wet mud in early spring. Named varieties do not come true from seed and must be divided to produce authentic plants.

Iris laevigata 'Variegata'

Water depth: 5-10cm (2-4in)
Height: 50-70cm (20-27in)
Description: Handsome plants with clumps of strongly variegated green-and-cream, sword-shaped leaves. Blue flowers appear during early to midsummer. This lovely plant is often sold as *Iris laevigata* 'Elegantissima'.
Propagation: Divide established plants immediately after flowering.

Iris pseudacorus
● Yellow flag

Water depth: Moist soil to 30cm (12in)
Height: 75-120cm (30-48in)
Description: A very vigorous plant that is unsuited to a small garden pool, but excellent for a wildlife water garden or planted alongside a stream. Tall, green, straplike leaves and bright yellow flowers with conspicuous black markings are produced during early to midsummer. *Iris pseudacorus* var. *bastardii* is less vigorous, with flowers of a more creamy yellow colour, and 'Flore Pleno' is double-flowered.
Propagation: Divide established plants immediately after flowering. The species can also be raised from seed sown in trays of mud in the spring.

Iris pseudacorus 'Variegatus'

Water depth: Moist soil to 15cm (6in)
Height: 60-90cm (24-36in)
Description: This is one of the best variegated aquatic plants. It produces handsome green-and-cream variegated, sword-shaped leaves that are very effective during spring and early summer. As the summer progresses, they begin to fade to pale green. Bright golden yellow flowers appear during early summer.
Propagation: Divide established plants immediately after flowering.

Iris versicolor 'Kermesina'

Water depth: Moist soil to 15cm (6in)
Height: 60-75cm (24-30in)
Description: A modest-growing, early to midsummer flowering iris that is ideal for a smaller pool. Rich plum-coloured blossoms are conspicuously marked with yellow, while the sword-shaped leaves are plain green.
Propagation: Sow seed in trays of mud in spring. Divide established plants immediately after flowering. This is the only method· of propagation for cultivars.

Above: There are a number of improved varieties of
the yellow flag (Iris pseudacorus). 'Golden Fleece' has
attractive bright yellow flowers that are devoid of any
markings, but it grows just as vigorously.

A selection of irises

Iris laevigata has sired many very fine aquatic varieties. They are available in a range of colours to suit every type of pond planting.

'Albopurpurea' purple and white
'Atropurpurea' reddish-purple
'Colchesterensis' white and dark blue
'Lilacina' light blue
'Midnight' deep blue, petals lined white
'Mottled Beauty' white mottled with pale blue
'Rose Queen' soft rose-pink
'Snowdrift' double-flowered white

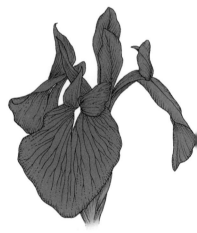

Iris laevigata
(above) is a reliable summer-flowering iris with clear blue blossoms above clumps of narrow, green swordlike leaves.

Iris laevigata *'Variegata'*
(left) has boldly variegated creamy white-and-green swordlike foliage and beautifully sculpted blue flowers.

Iris pseudacorus
(above) is a strong-growing iris with bright yellow flowers amongst broad, green swordlike leaves arising from a tough, creeping rootstock.

Iris pseudacorus 'Variegatus'
(above) has yellow flowers amongst bold yellow-cream and green striped sword-shaped leaves that pale to green as summer progresses.

Iris versicolor 'Kermesina'
(right) bears striking plum-coloured blossoms with yellow markings above narrow, green swordlike foliage during the summer.

Mentha aquatica
● Water mint

Water depth: Moist soil to 15cm (6in)
Height: 30-45cm (12-18in)
Description: An easily grown but vigorous marginal plant that is often used to disguise the edge of a water feature. A strongly aromatic plant with characteristic mint foliage on purple or reddish stems. Soft lilac-pink whorls of flowers appear in summer.
Propagation: Root stem cuttings in trays of mud in summer or divide creeping stems and rootstocks in early spring.

Menyanthes trifoliata
● Bog bean

Water depth: Moist soil to 15cm (6in)
Height: 20-30cm (8-12in)
Description: A very distinctive scrambling plant for shallow water. Showy white, fringed flowers are produced amongst dark green foliage that resembles the leaves of a broad bean plant. This is a very useful plant for disguising the harsh edge of a pool.
Propagation: Cut the sprawling stem into small sections, each with a bud, during early spring. Plant these in trays of mud.

Mimulus luteus
● Yellow musk

Water depth: Moist soil to 15cm (6in)
Height: 20-30cm (8-12in)
Description: A fast-growing, spreading plant with soft, green, rounded foliage. Spires of bright yellow flowers, rather like those of an antirrhinum, produce an excellent show for much of the summer. A free-seeding plant that can become a nuisance if not carefully controlled.
Propagation: Sow seed during early spring in a frame or unheated greenhouse, or divide the overwintered rosettes of foliage in early spring.

Mimulus ringens
● Blue musk

Water depth: Moist soil to 15cm (6in)
Height: 30-45cm (12-18in)
Description: A much-branched, slender-stemmed plant with narrow, bright green leaflets. The summer flowers are almost tubular, soft lavender to blue in colour and freely produced along a spiky stem.
Propagation: Sow seed during early spring on trays of mud in a cold frame, or root summer stem cuttings in mud. Mature plants can also be carefully divided in the spring.

Left: The yellow musk (Mimulus luteus) is very versatile and grown both in garden ponds and wildlife pools. It needs careful management as it seeds freely.

Right: The water forget-me-not (Myosotis scorpioides) is one of the most useful marginal plants, providing a summer-long display of attractive starry blue blossoms.

Myosotis scorpioides
● Water forget-me-not

Water depth: Moist soil to 15cm (6in)
Height: 15-20cm (6-8in)
Description: Rather like the traditional bedding forget-me-not in appearance, the water forget-me-not is a reliable perennial that will continue from year to year. It produces generous clumps of bright green foliage liberally sprinkled with light blue flowers. There is a vigorous seed-raised strain called 'Semperflorens' that has a more compact habit and is very free-flowering.
Propagation: Divide old plants in early spring, only retaining the young outer portions, or sow seed with the protection of a cold frame during spring.

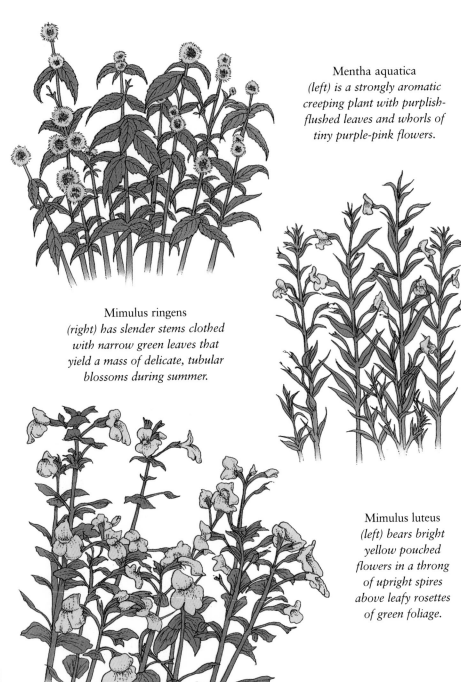

Mentha aquatica
*(left) is a strongly aromatic
creeping plant with purplish-
flushed leaves and whorls of
tiny purple-pink flowers.*

Mimulus ringens
*(right) has slender stems clothed
with narrow green leaves that
yield a mass of delicate, tubular
blossoms during summer.*

Mimulus luteus
*(left) bears bright
yellow pouched
flowers in a throng
of upright spires
above leafy rosettes
of green foliage.*

Menyanthes trifoliata *(right) produces clusters of delicately fringed white flowers from a scrambling tangle of dark green divided foliage during spring.*

Myosotis scorpioides *(below) has generous clumps of bright green foliage liberally sprinkled with small, starry, pale blue flowers in summer.*

Myriophyllum aquaticum *(below) has spreading whorls of beautiful feathery, pale green foliage that turns fiery red with the approach of autumn.*

Myriophyllum aquaticum
● Parrot's feather

Water depth: Up to 60cm (24in)
Description: A very popular, partially submerged, feathery foliage aquatic, with handsome, blue-green, finely cut leaves on scrambling stems. The foliage turns red during the autumn. In very cold regions, root a few shoots in late summer to take indoors in case of loss.
Propagation: Cuttings taken during the growing season root readily. Prepare bunches of three or four stems, fasten them together with a strip of lead and plant them in their permanent positions.

Below: Parrot's feather (Myriophyllum aquaticum) *is valuable for disguising the edges of artificial pools. It also provides a useful underplanting for tall growing marginals around the pond.*

Pontederia cordata
● Pickerel weed

Water depth: Moist soil to 15cm (6in)
Height: 60-90cm (24-36in)
A striking plant with glossy green, lance-shaped leaves and strong spikes of soft blue flowers during late summer. It makes an ideal companion for the flowering rush, *Butomus umbellatus*. White- and pink-flowered forms have been recently introduced to gardeners.
Propagation: Divide established plants once they start actively growing in the spring. Sow seed when it is still green in trays of mud during late summer.

Ranunculus lingua 'Grandiflora'
● Greater spearwort

Water depth: Moist soil to 15cm (6in)
Height: 60-90cm (24-36in)
Description: A tall-growing relative of the buttercup, with bright yellow, saucerlike

flowers during midsummer. Dark green foliage is carried on erect stems that are strongly flushed with rose, especially as the shoots emerge during early spring.
Propagation: Divide established plants in early spring.

Above: The pickerel weed (Pontederia cordata) *takes a season to become established, but then delights with its bright, glossy, green foliage and spikes of soft blue flowers during late summer.*

Sagittaria japonica
- Japanese arrowhead

Water depth: Moist soil to 15cm (6in)
Height: 45-60cm (18-24in)
Description: A tidy plant, with clumps of glossy, mid-green, arrow-shaped leaves and strong spikes of papery white, single flowers with yellow centres. The winter buds, or turions, are eaten by waterfowl.
Propagation: Divide growing clumps during the summer or redistribute the winter buds, or turions.

Sagittaria sagittifolia 'Flore Pleno'
- Double arrowhead

Water depth: Moist soil to 15cm (6in)
Height: 30-45cm (12-18in)
Description: A beautiful summer-flowering plant, with fully double white blossoms on strong spikes. These are produced from clumps of arrow-shaped foliage. Protect the overwintering buds, or turions, from waterfowl.
Propagation: Divide growing clumps during the summer or redistribute the winter buds, or turions.

Pontederia cordata
*(left) During mid- to
late summer, dense
spikes of soft blue
flowers appear from
stately, upright, glossy
green foliage.*

Ranunculus lingua
'*Grandiflora*'
*(right) A tall-growing
buttercup-like plant,
with dark green spear-
shaped leaves and
yellow saucerlike
flowers during
summer.*

Sagittaria japonica *(left) produces strong spikes of paper-white flowers with yellow centres above the distinctive, glossy, arrow-shaped foliage.*

Sagittaria sagittifolia *'Flore Pleno' (right) produces beautiful fully double white flowers on strong spikes from amongst clumps of arrow-shaped leaves during summer.*

Schoenoplectus lacustris tabernaemontani 'Albescens'

Water depth: Moist soil to 15cm (6in)
Height: 90-120cm (36-48in)
One of the loveliest rushes, with stout, upright, needlelike stems of glowing yellowish white, strongly marked with thin, longitudinal green stripes. The brownish flowers are produced in occasional small groups or tassels. Protect the plant from frost in very cold areas.
Propagation: Divide established clumps during the early spring.

Schoenoplectus lacustris tabernaemontani 'Zebrinus'
● Zebra rush

Water depth: Moist soil to 15cm (6in)
Height: 90cm (36in)
Description: A medium-sized rush with very distinctive needlelike foliage that is alternately barred with green and white. Occasional green shoots will appear; remove these before they swamp the desirable variegated part of the plant.
Propagation: Divide growing clumps during early spring.

Typha angustifolia
● Narrow-leaved reedmace

Water depth: Moist soil to 30cm (12in)
Height: 90-180cm (36-72in)
Description: This plant is popularly known as the bulrush, a handsome plant with tall, slender, grey-green foliage and bold brown pokerlike seedheads. It is only suitable for a larger or wildlife pool. The fruiting heads are often used for dried indoor decoration.
Propagation: Divide established plants during early spring.

Typha minima
● Dwarf Japanese reedmace

Water depth: Moist soil to 5cm (2in)
Height: 45cm (18in)
Description: A beautiful miniature reedmace for a small garden pool, tub or sink. A complete miniature, with green grassy foliage and chunky, rounded, dark brown seedheads. Unlike the other reedmaces, it is not at all invasive.
Propagation: Divide mature plants during early spring.

Veronica beccabunga
● Brooklime

Water depth: Moist soil to 15cm (6in)
Height: 15-20 cm (6-8in)
Description: A semi-evergreen marginal with trailing stems that are ideal for disguising the pool edge. The leaves are dark green, rounded and produced in abundance. Dark blue flowers, each with a white eye, are sprinkled over the plant for much of the summer.
Propagation: Root short stem cuttings in pans of mud at any time during the summer. The plant naturally roots freely along its creeping stems and pieces can be easily detached.

Right: Most gardeners want to enjoy the pokerlike heads of the narrow-leaved reedmace (Typha angustifolia) at their poolside, even though the plant requires careful controlling.

MARGINAL PLANTS

Veronica beccabunga *(left) is a semievergreen scrambling plant with green rounded leaves. Dark blue flowers with a white eye are produced during summer.*

Schoenoplectus lacustris tabernaemontani *'Albescens' (below) is a fine rush with upright needlelike stems of vivid yellowwhite with a longitudinal green stripe.*

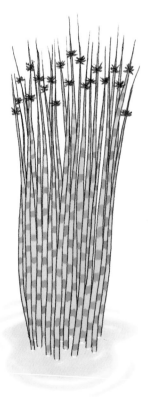

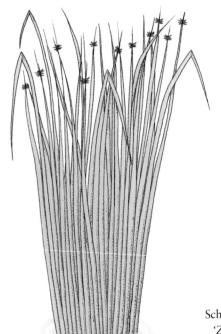

Schoenoplectus lacustris tabernaemontani *'Zebrinus' (above) is a very distinctive, needlelike rush. Its leaves are marked with alternate horizontal bands of green and white.*

Typha minima
*(below) produces
strong clumps of dark
green grassy foliage
that give rise to stems
with chunky dark
brown seedheads
during late summer.*

Typha angustifolia
*(above) produces thick, brown
pokerlike fruiting heads amongst
the tall, slender, grey-green
foliage during late summer.*

113

HARDY SUBMERGED PLANTS

The submerged plants are often erroneously referred to as oxygenating plants. While it is true that they provide oxygen for pond life, they are not unique in this respect. Their great virtue is their ability to utilise the nutrients otherwise exploited by water-discolouring algae.

Callitriche hermaphroditica
● Autumnal starwort

Water depth: Up to 45cm (18in)
Description: A completely submerged starwort with bright green, evergreen, cresslike foliage. Grows freely when water conditions are good, but often struggles in a newly made pool.
Propagation: Divide actively growing plants or remove stem cuttings during the summer and fasten bunches together with a strip of lead before planting them in their permanent positions.

Ceratophyllum demersum
● Hornwort

Water depth: Any, as it spends most of its life suspended freely in the water.
Description: A dark green, totally submerged plant with dense whorls of bristly foliage on brittle stems. For the most part, the plant floats just beneath the surface of the water, but in winter it retreats into turions, or winter buds.
Propagation: Separate the scrambling growths. For commercial purposes, ceratophyllum is usually sold in bunches tied with a lead weight.

Elodea canadensis
● Canadian pondweed

Water depth: Up to 120cm (48in)
Description: A vigorous submerged aquatic with small dark-green leaves arranged in very dense whorls along extensive branching stems. Almost evergreen and much loved by fish. Easy to control when grown in a basket.
Propagation: Fasten bunches of cuttings together with a narrow strip of lead and then plant them in their permanent positions. Only take cuttings in the active spring and summer growing seasons.

Fontinalis antipyretica
● Willow moss

Water depth: Up to 60cm (24in)
Description: A submerged aquatic with olive-green mosslike foliage that flourishes in moving water, although it is equally happy in still water. Much loved by fish as a spawning ground.
Propagation: Separate clumps during the growing season and replant them in their permanent positions. Vigorous young growth can be removed as cuttings during the summer months.

Above: A generous growth of hardy submerged aquatic, such as Lagarosiphon major, *ensures healthy, crystal clear water. However, do not allow it to take over the pond, as some open water is beneficial.*

115

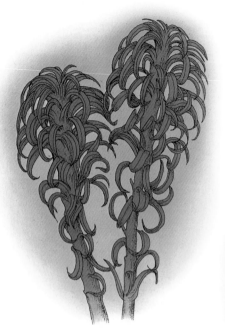

Lagarosiphon major (Elodea crispa)
*(left) has long, dark green,
scrambling, submerged stems
densely clothed with crispy foliage
that is much appreciated by fish.*

Fontinalis antipyretica *(right) has dense
masses of olive-green, mosslike foliage
that form a plant that is happy in both
fast-moving and still water.*

Ranunculus
aquatilis *(left)
produces white-
and-gold blossoms
just above water
level from amongst
deeply dissected,
fresh green
submerged foliage.*

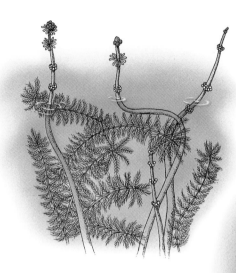

Myriophyllum spicatum
*(left) is a vigorous
submerged plant with
trailing stems of fine bronze-
green leaves and insignificant
red-and-yellow
flower spikes.*

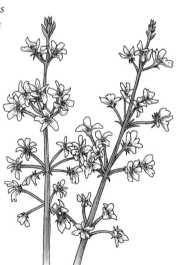

Potamogeton crispus
*(right) has handsome, translucent,
bronze-green, submerged foliage that
resembles seaweed, but the plant also
produces small crimson-and-yellow
emergent flower spikes.*

Ceratophyllum demersum
*(below) produces whorls
of dark green bristly
foliage on trailing stems
that usually float just
beneath the water surface.*

Hottonia palustris
*(below right) produces
beautiful spikes of off-
white or lilac blossoms
above the water from
delicate, pale green,
submerged foliage.*

Hottonia palustris
● Water violet

Water depth: Up to 60cm (24in)
Description: One of the finest submerged aquatics, producing handsome spikes of off-white or lilac blossoms above the water. The submerged foliage is bright green, finely divided and produced on stout stems. Towards the end of the season, the stems tend to break away from one another and much of the plant can be observed free-floating.
Propagation: Fasten summer cuttings together in bunches with a narrow strip of lead. Redistribute emerging winter turions in spring.

Lagarosiphon major
(Elodea crispa)
● Fish weed

Water depth: Up to 120cm (48in)
Description: Probably the best-known totally submerged aquatic plant. It produces long, succulent stems, densely clothed in dark green crispy foliage. It is one of the most versatile submerged plants, effectively controlling green water and much appreciated by fish.
Propagation: Fasten bunches of cuttings together with a narrow strip of lead and plant them in their permanent positions. Only remove cuttings during the active spring and summer growing season.

Left: Water crowfoot (Ranunculus aquatilis) grows equally well in both moving water and still. It is one of the few submerged aquatics which produces a creditable display of blossoms.

Myriophyllum spicatum
- Spiked milfoil

Water depth: Up to 90cm (36in)
Description: A popular submerged aquatic that produces small red-and-yellowish flower spikes above the surface of the water during summer. The ferny foliage is bronze-green and much loved by fish for spawning.
Propagation: Fasten bunches of cuttings together with a narrow strip of lead and plant them in their permanent positions. Only remove cuttings during the active spring and summer growing seasons.

Potamogeton crispus
- Curled pondweed

Water depth: Up to 90cm (36in)
Description: This freely-growing aquatic has bronze translucent foliage, rather like

Left: The water violet (Hottonia palustris) is a most beautiful submerged aquatic. However, it prospers in a well balanced environment and should only be planted in an established pond.

that of a seaweed. The leaves are crisped and crimped and borne on extensive succulent stems. The small crimson-and-yellow flower spikes are produced just above the water surface.
Propagation: Fasten bunches of cuttings together with a narrow strip of lead and plant them in their permanent positions. Only remove cuttings during the active spring and summer growing seasons.

Ranunculus aquatilis
- Water crowfoot

Water depth: Up to 90cm (36in)
Description: A most beautiful plant with deeply dissected submerged foliage. Just before flowering, it produces floating leaves reminiscent of clover. The cup-shaped blossoms, which appear during early summer, have papery white petals and golden centres and look like refined buttercup flowers.
Propagation: Fasten bunches of cuttings together with a narrow strip of lead and plant them in their permanent positions. Only remove cuttings during the active spring and summer growing seasons.

HARDY FLOATING PLANTS

Apart from their decorative merit, free-floating hardy aquatic plants serve a practical role in creating an ecological balance. They reduce the light levels beneath the water and make life intolerable for water-discolouring algae.

Azolla caroliniana
● Fairy moss

Description: A tiny floating fern with beautiful bluish-green or purplish-tinted lacy foliage. Although regarded as frost hardy, azolla disappears following a hard winter. In order to start a fresh colony the following spring, remove a portion towards the end of the growing season and place it in a bowl of water with a little soil on the bottom. Stand the bowl in a light, frost-free place.
Propagation: Separate and redistribute groups of floating foliage.

Hydrocharis morsus-ranae
● Frogbit

Description: A small floating plant that looks rather like a tiny waterlily. The small, bright green, kidney-shaped leaves are produced in neat rosettes. The three-petalled, papery flowers are white with conspicuous yellow centres and appear during summer. The frogbit produces turions, or winter buds, which fall to the bottom of the pool for the winter and start growing again in spring.
Propagation: Separate out plantlets as individuals during the growing season.

Lemna minor
● Lesser duckweed

Description: Like all duckweeds, this one can be invasive. It is often introduced to wildlife pools or where fish are the main interest, as the tiny, pale green, rounded leaflets are much enjoyed by goldfish.
Propagation: Separate and redistribute groups of floating foliage.

Stratiotes aloides
● Water soldier

Description: An interesting floating aquatic that looks rather like a pineapple top. During the summer it produces creamy-white papery flowers in its leaf axils. The water soldier usually overwinters as a dormant winter bud or small plantlet.
Propagation: Separate and detach young plants from runners that are produced during the growing season.

Right: The frogbit (Hydrocharis morsus-ranae) is a charming small floating plant that is well suited to life in a tub or sink. It flowers freely throughout the summer.

Trapa natans
● Water chestnut

Description: A handsome plant with rosettes of dark green, rhomboidal leaves and pretty white axillary flowers during mid- to late summer. An annual that seeds itself freely. Even when the nuts are not gathered, sufficient are usually deposited on the floor of the pool to ensure fresh plants for the following year.
Propagation: Gather ripe nuts and place them in a bowl of water with some soil on the bottom. They will overwinter and start into growth again in the spring.

Utricularia vulgaris
● Greater bladderwort

Description: A curious floating plant with spikes of showy, bright yellow flowers, not unlike those of an antirrhinum, but rather smaller. These are produced above a tangle of dainty, dull green, lacy foliage that has tiny bladders distributed throughout. These capture aquatic insect life, which the plant digests. The plant forms turions, or winter buds, which fall to the bottom of the pool.
Propagation: Redistribute the tangled mass of foliage during the summer.

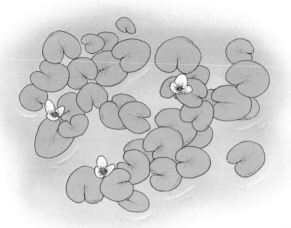

Hydrocharis
morsus-ranae
*(left) forms colonies
of kidney-shaped,
bright green leaves
and produces simple,
three-petalled,
white papery
flowers.*

Trapa natans
*(right) has dark
green rhomboidal
leaves that form
neat, floating
rosettes from which
pretty white flowers
are produced.*

Stratiotes aloides
*(left) has olive green
foliage reminiscent
of a pineapple top.
Creamy-white,
papery flowers are
produced from the
leaf junctions.*

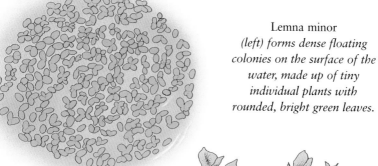

Lemna minor
(left) forms dense floating
colonies on the surface of the
water, made up of tiny
individual plants with
rounded, bright green leaves.

Utricularia vulgaris
(right) has short spikes
of bright yellow
blossoms held above the
water, arising from a
tangle of deeply divided
green foliage.

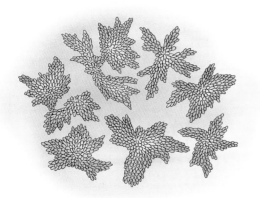

Azolla caroliniana
(left), a beautiful
floating fern with
dainty, green,
filigree foliage, often
rose or purplish
tinted, that forms
spreading colonies.

123

Bog Garden Plants

Bog garden plants are those that enjoy permanently damp conditions, but will not tolerate standing in water, especially during the winter. By careful selection they can extend the season of poolside interest.

Astilbe
* False goat's beard

Height: 30-90cm (12-36in)
Description: The astilbes are attractive plants of neat habit with dark green, deeply divided foliage and handsome plumes of blossom. 'Fanal', which grows to 30-40cm/12-16in, is the finest of the red varieties. *A.* x *rosea* 'Peach Blossom' (60-90cm/24-36in) is salmon pink, and 'White Gloria' (60-75cm/24-30in) is the loveliest compact white.
Propagation: Divide established plants during the winter dormant period. Only replant the young vigorous growths from the outer portion of each clump.

Filipendula
* Meadowsweet

Height: 50-120cm (20-48in)
Description: There is a wide range of filipendulas with dense, feathery spires of often sweetly scented tiny blossoms of pink, red, cream and white. The leaves are dark green, deeply cut and spreading.
Propagation: Divide established plants during the dormant winter period. Always replant smaller young divisions. Woody material is unsatisfactory.

Hosta
* Plantain lily

Height: 30-75cm (12-30in)
Description: Wonderful foliage plants with oval or lance-shaped green, gold, blue-green or variegated leaves. The tubular blossoms are lavender or white and borne freely on slender stems. Hostas are much loved by slugs and this should be taken into account when placing them in the bog garden.
Propagation: Divide established plants in early spring as soon as the shoots are starting to show through the soil.

Iris ensata
* Clematis-flowered iris of Japan or Japanese water iris

Height: 60-90cm (24-36in)
Description: This beautiful bog iris will not tolerate alkaline soil or standing water during the winter. The species has tufts of broad, grassy or narrow, swordlike foliage and soft, velvety deep-purple blossoms. There are many named varieties, including 'Blue Skies' (60-75cm 24-30in); 'Landscape at Dawn' (60-75cm 24-30in) a pale rose lavender; and 'Variegata' (60cm/24in), with simple

Above: *Astilbes and bog garden irises crowd at the poolside. A bog area creates a wonderful opportunity for adding colour and both foliage and form to the water garden.*

Right: Filipendula vulgaris *is an easily grown swamp plant, ideally suited to the wildlife pond. It is sweetly scented and attracts a multitude of butterflies and other small insects. There are a number of garden varieties in a range of colours.*

violet-blue flowers and the most striking cream-and-green striped foliage. The Higo strain is the best of the hybrid mixtures.

Propagation: Mixtures of *Iris ensata* can be easily raised from seed sown during spring in a good-quality, lime-free potting mix in trays in a cold frame. Propagate named varieties by division in summer immediately flowering is over.

Iris sibirica
● Siberian iris

Height: 60-90cm (24-36in)

Description: A very versatile bog garden plant that tolerates dry conditions reasonably, as well as periodic inundation with water. It is therefore an ideal plant for the streamside. Elegant pale blue blossoms on strong erect stems emerge from vigorous tufts of grassy foliage. There are many good varieties, including 'Emperor' (90cm/36in), a deep violet-purple; 'Perry's Blue' (90cm/36in), which is sky-blue; and 'Perry's Pigmy' (45cm/18in), a deep violet-blue.

Propagation: The species can be raised from seed sown in trays filled with a soil-based seed mixture. Sow the seed in a cold frame during early spring. Propagate named varieties by division immediately after flowering.

Lobelia

Height: 60-90cm (24-36in)

Description: Although mostly winter hardy, in very cold areas it is prudent to overwinter one or two plants of these lovely bog garden perennials in a cold frame or unheated greenhouse.

There are several kinds, including the red-flowered, purple-leaved 'Queen Victoria' and the purple-flowered, green-leaved *L.* 'Vedrariensis'. The blue-blossomed *L. siphilitica* and its white form are very hardy.

Propagation: Divide the overwintered rosettes in early spring. Pot them up so that they can establish a good root system before being planting out in their permanent positions in late spring or early summer.

Above: Perennial lobelias provide vivid summer colour. In cold districts some varieties are considered half-hardy, but they are easy to overwinter in a cold frame or unheated greenhouse.

Left: The Siberian iris *(*Iris sibirica*)*, and its many varieties are reliable bog garden plants. They prosper in the rough and tumble of the streamside as well as the calm of the garden pool.

Lysichiton americanus
● American skunk cabbage

Height: 60-90cm (24-36in)
Description: A hardy relative of the arum lily, but with much larger, bright yellow flowers that appear long before the cabbagelike foliage. There is a white-flowered skunk cabbage with smaller flowers that comes from Asia and is called *L. camtschatcensis*.
Propagation: Sow ripe seed immediately in soil-based mix in a plastic seed tray with drainage holes. Stand this tray inside a larger, unperforated one filled with water, and keep it in a cold frame.

127

Lysichiton americanus (left) has striking bright yellow spathes of flowers during spring before the large cabbagelike green leaves appear.

Lysimachia nummularia (right) is a more-or-less evergreen scrambling plant that is smothered in small, yellow, buttercup-like flowers during the summer.

Primula *candelabra* hybrids (left) produce tiered whorls of brightly coloured blossoms above fresh green, cabbagelike leaves during late spring and early summer.

Hosta
*'Thomas Hogg'
(left) produces
clumps of beautiful
green leaves with
distinctive creamy
white-edged foliage
and occasional
spikes of purplish
violet, bell-shaped
flowers.*

Iris ensata
*(below) has large, beautifully
formed, clematis-like blossoms in
blue, purple, rose or white amongst
narrow, green, sword-shaped leaves.*

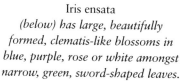

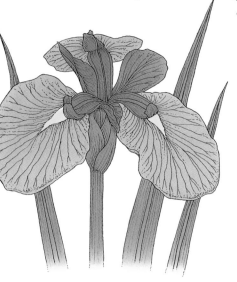

Astilbe arendsii
*(right) is a compact-growing plant with
deeply divided foliage and feathery
plumes of red, pink or white blossoms.*

129

Right: Mimulus luteus has given rise to a wide range of colourful garden varieties of musk that all flourish in damp soil or the poolside margins. This one is 'Queen's Prize'.

Lysimachia nummularia
● Creeping Jenny

Height: 5cm (2in)
Description: A more or less evergreen carpeting plant that is often used to disguise the awkward edge between the pool and the surrounding ground. For much of the summer the plant is studded with bright yellow, buttercup-like flowers. A golden-leaved cultivar, *L. n.* 'Aurea', also has yellow flowers.
Propagation: Take short stem cuttings at any time during the summer growing period. This plant usually layers itself freely and the rooted pieces can be severed and lifted at any time.

Mimulus hybrids

Height: 20-30cm (8-12in)
Description: Beautiful plants with multi-coloured blossoms that are often attractively splashed and spotted with red or maroon. Soft green succulent foliage provides a perfect foil for the exotic-looking flowers. Although they are perennial plants, modern hybrids are best raised annually from seed.
Propagation: Sow seed in a tray or pan of good-quality seed mixture during early spring and germinate it in a warm greenhouse or near a window. Prick out the young seedlings and pot them on individually to produce good sturdy plants for planting out in early summer.

Left: The globe flower, or trollius, is one of the hardiest and earliest flowering bog garden plants. It has given rise to a fine range of named varieties.

Primula

Height: 25-90cm (10-36in)
Description: There is a range of primulas for boggy conditions, mostly with candelabra or pendant heads of colourful flowers. There are species and varieties that will flower variously from early spring until late summer. All make a striking show and are reliably hardy.
Propagation: Divide established plants during the early spring, just as the leafy shoots are emerging. Sow seed immediately it ripens in a good-quality seed mixture with the protection of a cold frame.

Trollius
● Globe flower

Height: 30-45cm (12-18in)
Description: Attractive, globular flowers of rich golden yellow or orange are produced on strong wiry stems above compact mounds of finely toothed foliage. There are several named kinds, such as the reddish-orange 'Fireglobe', orange 'Orange Globe' and canary yellow 'Earliest of All'.
Propagation: Divide established plants during the dormant winter period and immediately plant out the divisions in their permanent positions.

Over: Bog garden primulas establish well at the poolside and provide bright colour from early spring until late summer. The candelabra species and varieties are some of the most showy and are at their best during late spring.

INDEX

O

P

R

Y

Z

CREDITS

The practical photographs featured in this book have been taken by Geoffrey Rogers and are © Interpet Publishing.

The publishers would like to thank the following photographers for providing images, credited here by page number and position: B(Bottom), T(Top), C(Centre), BL(Bottom Left), etc.

Biofotos (Heather Angel): 68
Eric Crichton: 10, 19(TR), 20, 23, 46-47, 54, 74, 106, 115, 125(T), 127, 130(B), 132-133
The Garden Picture Library: 12(Brigitte Thomas), 22(Juliette Wade), 25(Mayer/Le Scanff), 27(Howard Rice), 29(Gary Rogers), 30(T, John Miller), 35(T, John Glover), 35(B, Friedrich Strauss), 91(Brian Carter)
John Glover: 33, 81
Jerry Harpur: 34(BR)
Sunniva Harte: 21(BL, Terry Hill), 30(B)
S & O Mathews: 16, 24, 36, 49, 88, 119, 126
Clive Nichols: 14-15(B. Greenhurst Garden, Sussex)
Photos Horticultural: 69, 125(B)
Geoffrey Rogers: 28, 70, 71, 72, 95, 102, 103, 130(T)
Neil Sutherland © Geoffrey Rogers: Copyright page, 18, 21(R), 76, 78, 80, 85, 87, 99, 107, 111, 121

The artwork illustrations have been prepared by Guy Smith, Mainline Design, Maidstone, Kent and are © Interpet Publishing.

ACKNOWLEDGMENTS

Thanks are due to Anthony Archer-Wills; The Dorset Water Lily Company, Halstock, Dorset; Neales Aquatic Nurseries, West Kingsdown, Kent; Tetra (UK) and Washington Garden Centre, West Sussex for their help in the preparation of this book.